河之北

世界文化遗产

NORTH OF THE GREAT RIVER
World Cultural Heritage

大型纪录片《大河之北》项目组　编著

河北出版传媒集团
河北教育出版社

图书在版编目（CIP）数据

大河之北：世界文化遗产 / 大型纪录片《大河之北》
项目组编著. —— 石家庄：河北教育出版社，2023.9
　　ISBN 978-7-5545-7570-3

　　Ⅰ.①大… Ⅱ.①大… Ⅲ.①文化遗产 – 介绍 – 河北
Ⅳ.①G127.22

　　中国国家版本馆CIP数据核字(2023)第012468号

书　　名　大河之北 世界文化遗产
　　　　　DAHE ZHI BEI SHIJIE WENHUA YICHAN
编　　著　大型纪录片《大河之北》项目组
策　　划　丁　伟
出 版 人　董素山
责任编辑　汪雅瑛　陈　娟
英文编辑　刘艳花　王丹宏
装帧设计　郝　旭

出版发行　河北出版传媒集团
　　　　　河北教育出版社　http://www.hbep.com
　　　　　（石家庄市联盟路705号，050061）
印　　制　河北鹏润印刷有限公司
开　　本　787毫米×1092毫米　　1/16
印　　张　20.5
字　　数　200千字
版　　次　2023年9月第1版
印　　次　2023年9月第1次印刷
书　　号　ISBN 978-7-5545-7570-3
定　　价　188.00元

世界文化遗产

《大河之北》系列图书编委会

主　任	武鸿儒				
副 主 任	李社军				
编　委	王成树	朱　新	许伟中	王　东	孙卓理
文字采编	张晓雯	刘振江	冬　清	刘亚楠	杨之行　辛七天
	刘　婷	解　伟	李　辉	陈明岩	张　剑　左　钊
	王润沛	杨雪健	谭　杰		
撰　稿	张晓雯				
翻　译	李正栓	吕伟利	傅花道		
摄　影	刘振江	田银龙	杨　东	贾　磊	李岩峰　刘国旭
	邹月光	张志朋	文　明	李连杰	

大河之北 是我故乡

刘海儒

习近平总书记在正定工作时，曾在《中国青年》杂志上发表题为《知之深 爱之切》的文章。他说："要热爱自己的家乡，首先要了解家乡。深厚的感情必须以深刻的认识做基础。唯有对家乡知之甚深，才能爱之愈切。"

河北，北依燕山，南望黄河，西凭太行，东接沃野，内环京津，外沿渤海。这是中国唯一兼有高原、山地、丘陵、平原、湖泊和海滨的省份，被誉为"浓缩的国家地理读本"。

中华文明，犹如一条波澜壮阔的长河，奔流不息。齐全的地貌，决定了河北丰富多样的生产生活方式；独特的区位，又使得它的面貌和身份不停地变更。河北的山川见证了中国历史的变迁，历经了中华文化的发展。一路走来，这里留下了无数影响中国历史发展进程的精彩瞬间。

领略河北，感知河北，爱上河北，是每一个燕赵儿女的本分，更是媒体人肩负的责任和使命。如何从丰富多样的地理广度寻找这片土地于民族融合发展的独特意义，从源远流长的历史连续性来解读这片土地于中华文明的贡献，让大家既了解河北的过去，又理解河北的现在，从而更加坚信河北的未来，这是我们策划拍摄系列纪录片《大河之北》的初衷。为此，我们提出：要打造一部经得起历史检验的纪录片，记录时代变迁，讲好河北故事。

感谢所有参与这部作品创作的同志们，特别是我台精品创作中心主创团队，他们走遍山水，抢抓拍摄时机，克服重重困难，精益求精，于2021年初完成《大河之北》第一季"山川地理"。作品一经推出，便引发社会各界的广泛好评。随后我们一鼓作气，再接再厉，聚焦河北境内四项世界文化遗产，策划推出了《大河之北》之"世界文化遗产"；完成了讲述河北古往今来社会经济发展成就与贡献的《大河之北》之"生生不息"；摄制了反映河北文化底蕴、历代文明成果的《大河之北》之"文华燕赵"。

以古开今，鉴往知来。作为第一部全景式反映河北人文历史、地形地貌、丰饶物产的纪录片，四季24集1400余分钟的《大河之北》，展示了河北得天独厚的地理环境、重信尚义的民俗民风、丰富多彩的艺术文化、多元开放的经济脉落以及慷慨悲歌的人文精神。大河之北，是我故乡。通过解读燕赵大地的地域特点和开拓进取的基因，探析中华文明生生不息的密码，彰显中华民族的文化自信。

华章流韵，守正创新。如今，以这部系列纪录片为蓝本的大型系列图书《大河之北》编辑出版，这是作品呈现的一个新方式，也为朋友们提供了解河北的一个新渠道。不妥之处，还望大家批评指正。

（作者系中共河北省委宣传部副部长、河北广播电视台台长）

纪录片主创名单

出 品 人　武鸿儒

总 策 划　宋文新　武鸿儒　那书晨　王离湘

总 监 制　李社军　王振儒　王荣丽　李　丽　王成树

总制片人　李社军

策　　划　孙　雷　郭英朝　李新杰　甄玉峰

监　　制　朱　新　王　东

顾　　问　梁　勇　董耀会　杨国钧　周余良　李　专　赵英健　李　寅　杜志平　冯公禧

总 导 演　朱　新

执行总导演／总撰稿　张晓雯

执行总导演／制片人　刘振江

导　　演　冬　清　刘亚楠　辛七天　杨之行

解　　说　李立宏

宣传统筹　乔晓曦　葛晓宇　王　东

宣传推广　谷霄燕　刘　婷　解　伟　李　辉　张　剑　吕伟利　高卫平　范宝臣　谭　颖　刘　郦
　　　　　张国华　刘长亮　马玉竹　张振峰　马宁宁　谭　杰　布肃琦　郭育卿　杨兆歆　刘　然

出　　品　中共河北省委宣传部
　　　　　河北省文化和旅游厅
　　　　　河北省广播电视局
　　　　　河北广播电视台

摄　　影	刘国旭	杨　东	李彦峰	田银龙
	贾　磊	安晓光	曹轶明	张志朋
	邹月光	张春元	李文惠	王　建
	徐贺齐	王利军	李　奇	高金亮
航空拍摄	刘振江	杨华波	张志朋	李佳润
	柳　旸	贾　磊	段　林	李文惠
	王　建	徐贺齐	关嘉鑫	王利军
	陶洪飞			
延时拍摄	文　明	路　杰	贾　磊	裴复隆
	邹月光	李佳润	段林佳	李文惠
	邱　伟	周　健	关嘉鑫	
灯　　光	田银龙	王　江	唐玉珠	裴复隆
	郑时光	王　伟	赵云平	
摄影助理	李豆豆	范江鑫	赵家兴	宋鹏展
	苗晓宽	王　江	许立军	于赛超
	王雨晨	刘俊强	宋利乐	范江鑫
	赵家兴	刘金赛	赵云平	马玉垚
	周　健	沈玉航		
外　　联	张晓雯	王　雷	杨雪健	杨　燕
剪　　辑	贾煜资	康刘飒	邱伟帅	冬　清
	张立巍	康佳瑶	辛七天	王京波
	高　思	闫雨宁	邱　伟	甘林红

包　　装	甄天龙	李　煊	庞美婷	周　婷
	周韶光	张丽霞	鲍岩民	仇成博
	李亚松	萧竣元	孙晓光	王京波
	王晓松			
调　　色	朱海萌	康刘飒	邱伟帅	周韶光
	王京波	张立巍		
三维设计	王京波	孟　涛	孙晓光	李　煊
片头字幕	刘国旭			
技术统筹	梁　栋	李　悦		
录　　音	李　冕			
主题音乐作曲	陈　颖			
音乐编辑	陈　颖			
音效编辑	宋凯宇	赵煜东	张宜初	
成片混音	芶天禹			
制作统筹	杨　珮	李　娟		
播出统筹	王宇彤	程孟振	许伟中	杨素强
播出监制	冀国锋	罗大成	张雪梅	张勇军
	宋　超	王　磊	冯迎晖	
财务总监	戎增栓	齐赞九	陈　彤	
技术监制	杜立喜	孙　力		

目 录
Contents

1

North of the Great River: World Cultural Heritage

The Great Wall

长城

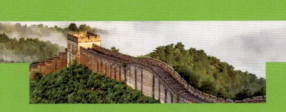

长城是其中最为古老的一项。从公元前七世纪开始，中国人倚傍山川地势，以人工增益天工，在两千多年的岁月里，修筑出人类历史上最长的一道军事防御工程，在天地间勾画出雄奇峻美的壮怀激烈。

长城的总长度几经变化，全部加起来超过了五万公里。险关要隘、雄浑逶迤，它是砖石筑就的传奇，更是中华民族意志与力量的图腾。

在河北境内，如今留存着大约两千五百千米长城，保存最完整、建筑最雄伟、文化最丰富的精华地段也留在了河北。

在漫长的演进历程中，人类凭借着非凡的大脑与勤劳的双手创造出诸多伟大的成就，而这其中最杰出的有形部分被誉为世界文化遗产。它们承载着世界历史悠长的发展脉络，彰显着人类文明的无限魅力，并在漫长的岁月里源源不断地为人们提供强大的精神动力。

In the long course of evolution, humankind has made many great achievements with their extraordinary brains and industrious hands. The most outstanding tangible part is honored as world cultural heritage. It carries the long course of development in world history, manifests the infinite charm of human civilization, and provides people with a strong intellectual impetus continuously in the long history.

这些闪耀于人类历史的世界文化遗产，有四项与河北这片土地有关：长城、大运河、避暑山庄及周围寺庙、清东西陵。

Among these world cultural heritages shining in human history, four sites are related to Hebei: the Great Wall, the Grand Canal, Chengde Mountain Resort and its surrounding temples, and the Eastern and Western Royal Tombs of the Qing Dynasty.

　　长城是其中最为古老的一项。从公元前七世纪开始，中国人倚傍山川地势，以人工增益天工，在两千多年的岁月里，修筑出人类历史上最长的一道军事防御工程，在天地间勾画出雄奇峻美的壮怀激烈。

The Great Wall is the time-honored heritage. Since the 7th century BC, relying on the terrain of mountains and rivers and adding to the work of nature with human efforts, the Chinese people have built the longest military defense project in human history in more than two thousand years, and have drawn a magnificent and beautiful picture of lofty aspiration between heaven and earth.

　　长城的总长度几经变化，全部加起来超过了5000千米。险关要隘、雄浑迤逦，它是砖石筑就的传奇，更是中华民族意志与力量的图腾。

The total length of the Great Wall has changed several times, adding up to more than 5,000 kilometers. With dangerous and strategic passes, it is vigorous and firm, winding on the mountains. It is not only a legend built with bricks and stones, but also a totem of the will and strength of the Chinese nation.

　　在河北境内，如今留存着大约2500千米长城，保存最完整、建筑最雄伟、文化最丰富的精华地段也留在了河北。

In Hebei, there are about 2,500 kilometers of the Great Wall today. The most intact, majestic and culturally-loaded sections of the Great Wall are in Hebei.

世界文化遗产

太行山，是横亘在华北平原与黄土高原之间的一道天然屏障。山中众多幽深的峡谷是穿越屏障的通道，道道周围的断陷盆地便是历代屯兵设关的军事重地。

The Taihang Mountains are a natural barrier between the North China Plain and the Loess Plateau. Many deep canyons in the mountains are the passages through the barrier. The graben basin around the passages has been key military strongholds for stationing troops and setting up passes in ancient dynasties.

河北省保定市涞源县就位于太行山脉的断陷盆地中，春秋战国时期，这里是燕、赵、中山三大诸侯国的必争之地。

Laiyuan County in Hebei Province's Baoding City is located in the graben basin of the Taihang Mountains. During the Spring and Autumn Period and Warring States Period, it was a place of strategic importance to the three Vassal States of Yan, Zhao and Zhongshan.

涞源黄土岭村东北边的山岭上逶迤着一道长约6000米的土墙，几乎与山融为一体。两千三百多年的雨雪风霜，让它的面目模糊而骨骼依旧。《史记·赵世家》记载，公元前369年，"中山筑长城"。在燕、赵两大强国之间求生存，中山全力自保，在今天的保定市境内修建了一道不足90千米的长城，这是河北境内已知修筑年代最早的长城。

On the mountain ridge on the northeast of Huangtuling Village of Laiyuan County, there is a 6,000-meter-long earthen wall. It is almost integrated with the mountain. The erosion of 2300 years by rain, snow, wind and frost blurred its features while the skeleton of the wall is still there. According to *the Hereditary House of Zhao in Records of the Grand Historian*, "the Great Wall was built in Zhongshan" in 369 BC. In order to survive between the two great powers of Yan and Zhao, Zhongshan State spared no effort to protect itself by building a Great Wall of less than 90 kilometers on the land of present Baoding City. It is the earliest Great Wall known in Hebei.

世界文化遗产

中山长城已有了后世长城的模样，配套建有烽燧和屯军之城。烽燧是长城的主要标志之一，它的出现早于长城。公元前九世纪建立的西周，在边境线上修筑夯土高台传递军情，以防外族侵扰。日间点燃以烟报警的叫燧，夜间点燃以火为号的是烽。烽火可以在一天之内横越1000千米，发出警报。

The Great Wall of Zhongshan State had the look of the Great Wall of later generations, with beacon towers (Feng Sui) and garrison places. The beacon tower is one of the main symbols of the Great Wall, yet it appeared earlier than the Great Wall. The Western Zhou Dynasty, which was founded in the 9th century BC, built rammed earthen platforms along the border to convey military messages and prevent invasion. The beacon fire lit to give an alarm by smoke during the day is called Sui, and lit to give border alarm by fire at night is called Feng. The beacon fire can travel 1,000 kilometers within a day to report the alarm.

烽燧还有另一个广为人知的名字，烽火台。这个名称随着"烽火戏诸侯"的故事流传至今。西周末代君王周幽王为博得美人褒姒一笑，点燃烽火台，戏弄诸侯。当危险真正来临时，诸侯们不再营救。一笑倾国，西周灭亡。

The beacon fire is also well-known as beacon tower, a name which has been passed so far along with the story of "Teasing the Dukes with Beacon". King You of Zhou, the last king of the Western Zhou Dynasty, lit the beacon tower to poke fun at the dukes and princes in order to win a smile of the beauty Baosi. When danger really came, the dukes and princes no longer tried to rescue them. A smile cost the collapse of Western Zhou Dynasty.

春秋战国时期，北部诸侯国与游牧民族比邻而居。游牧军队飘忽不定的行踪和迅疾猛烈的攻击让中原诸国无从招架。于是，燕、赵等国开始用长墙将烽火台加以连接，以期阻挡住北方的马蹄。出于划分边界与保护自己的需要，各诸侯国之间也筑起一道道长墙。长城，从此进入了中国的主流叙事。

In the Spring and Autumn Period and the Warring States Period, the northern vassal states and the nomadic people lived as neighbors. The erratic movements of the nomadic armies and their swift and fierce attacks left the central plains states helpless. Therefore, the States of Yan, Zhao and others began to connect beacon towers by long walls in order to block the horses hooves from the north. The vassal states also built long walls out of the need to demarcate boundaries and protect themselves. Since then the Great Wall has entered the mainstream narrative of China.

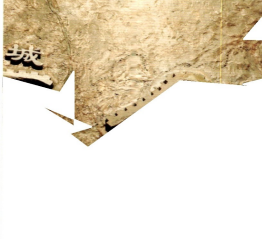

从秦代到明代，两千多年里，二十多个朝代都曾大规模修建长城。

From the Qin Dynasty to the Ming Dynasty, there were large-scale constructions of the Great Wall in more than twenty dynasties over two thousand years.

在京津冀地区，历代长城总是修建在自然、气候与地理环境的分界带上，基本与400毫米等降水线一致。巧合的背后其实是自然选择。这一地区长城的南侧是半干旱地区，植被多为林地草原，农业经济以种植业为主；北侧则是干旱地区，被草原与荒漠所覆盖，占优势的是牧业生产。

In Beijing-Tianjin-Hebei region, the Great Wall has always been built along the demarcation line of nature, climate and geographical environment, basically consistent with the 400mm equipluve line. It is a selection rather natural than coincidental. The southern side of the Great Wall in this area is semi-arid region, where the vegetation is mostly forest land and grassland, and the agricultural economy is based on farm production; the northern side is arid region, which is covered by grassland and desert, with livestock production as the dominant industry.

　　河北，横跨农牧两大地理环境，历史上，游牧民族与农耕民族在这里轮番上演着和平与纷争、繁荣与衰落。于是，长城选择了河北，在一砖一石的堆砌中，筑成了最坚固最精彩的一段。

　　Hebei stretches across two geographical environments of agriculture and animal husbandry. In history, there were peace and war, prosperity and decline between the nomadic and farming people. Therefore, the Great Wall chose Hebei, and the most solid and splendid section was built in the piling up of bricks and stones.

公元前221年，秦始皇统一中国。为防范北方草原的势力，他将燕、赵、秦三国的旧长城修缮连接，并增修新的长城。七年后，一条西起陇西，东到辽东的长城完工，这是第一条名副其实的万里长城。

In 221 BC, the First Emperor of the Qin Dynasty unified China. In order to prevent the forces from the northern grassland, he repaired and connected the old Great Walls of the States of Yan, Zhao and Qin, and built new walls. Seven years later, a Great Wall was completed, stretching from Longxi in the west to Liaodong in the east, which was known as the first Great Wall true to the name.

河北境内的秦长城大多存留在张家口与承德北部一带，长度超过460千米。在历代的改扩建与岁月的洗礼中，秦长城多数已经湮没在尘埃里，但一个关于长城的故事却在历史中沉淀下来，穿越时空直触人心。

Most of the Great Wall of the Qin Dynasty in Hebei Province are in the northern part of Zhangjiakou and Chengde, with a length of more than 460 kilometers. Through reconstruction and expansion of past dynasties in the long history, most of the Great Wall of the Qin Dynasty has been lost in the dust, but a story about the Great Wall has passed down in history, touching people's heart through time and space.

山海关旁有座凤凰山，凤凰山上有座庙，一千五百年来，这座庙宇和着渤海的潮起潮落诉说着一个悲情的故事。孟姜女的新婚丈夫范喜良被官府强征修建长城，两人生离死别。孟姜女万里寻夫，却只得白骨。她失声痛哭，其情感天动地，倾倒了长城。

There is a Mount Phoenix next to Shanhaiguan Pass, and there is a temple on the Mount. For 1500 years, the temple has been telling a tragic story with the ebb and flow of the tides in Bohai Sea. Fan Xiliang, Mengjiangnv's newlywed husband, was forced to build the Great Wall by the government, and they were separated like parting forever which proved true. Mengjiangnv went thousands of miles to search for her husband only to find his bones. She lost control and cried loudly. Even the heaven and the earth were touched. As a result, a part of the Great Wall collapsed.

打通河西走廊的汉代，修成了一条西起大宛贰师城，东至黑龙江北岸，全长近10000千米的长城，古丝绸之路有一半的路程就沿着这条长城。

During the Han Dynasty when Hexi Corridor was opened, the Great Wall was built from Ershi City in the State of Dayuan in the west to the northern bank of the Heilongjiang River in the east, with a total length of nearly 10,000 kilometers, and half of the ancient Silk Road ran along this Great Wall.

汉长城有250多千米经过张家口与承德。在张家口市尚义县的牛家营村与小蒜沟村，仍有清晰可辨的汉长城遗址。夯土的长墙随着平缓的山势起伏，烽火台兀立于山势险峻之处，静默凝重，依稀可以窥见汉长城的雄伟，"五里一燧、十里一墩、三十里一堡、百里一城"。

The Great Wall of the Han Dynasty passes through Zhangjiakou and Chengde for more than 250 kilometers. In Niujiaying Village and Xiaosuangou Village in Shangyi County of Zhangjiakou City, there are still clearly identifiable ruins of the Great Wall of the Han Dynasty. The long wall of rammed earth rises and falls with the gentle mountains, with beacon towers standing upright in the steep mountains, silent and imposing. The grandeur of the Great Wall of the Han Dynasty can be vaguely seen, with "every five li a beacon, ten li a mound, thirty li a walled-village, and one hundred li a city".

大境门 世界文化遗产

公元1368年，元朝统治者被迫退回草原，明朝建立。不甘失败的蒙古大军始终怀有再次南下的梦想。面对北方强敌的觊觎，明朝自然不会束手待毙。公元1421年，明成祖朱棣将都城从南京迁往北京，"天子守国门"，既是万全之策也是无奈之举。

In 1368, the rulers of the Yuan Dynasty were forced to retreat to the steppe and the Ming Dynasty was established. The Mongol army, who refused to resign themselves to defeat, had always been dreaming of marching south again. In the face of the powerful enemy in the north, the Ming Dynasty would not wait for death. In 1421, Zhu Di, Emperor Chengzu of the Ming Dynasty, moved the capital from Nanjing to Beijing: "The Emperor guards the country". It was a completely safe plan, yet he had no choice.

很快，为了长治久安，明廷开始修筑边墙。边墙就是长城，这项工程从明朝建立就着手进行。

Soon, in order to maintain the long-term stability of the country, the Government of the Ming Dynasty began to build side walls. The side wall is actually the Great Wall, the construction of which had been going on since the establishment of the Ming Dynasty.

　　仿佛倾注了整个王朝的和平希望与安定梦想，明廷对长城的重视无以复加。历史学家黄仁宇曾估算，明朝修1千米长城，一般花费7700两白银，高则31500两，总长6300千米的明长城，至少花费4850万两白银。可就算是财政黄金时期，明廷一年的收入也不过400万两白银。大手笔的投入带来立竿见影的效果，明长城的建造达到新的巅峰。

　　It seems that the whole dynasty places all its hope for peace and dream of stability on the Grea Wall, to which the Ming Dynasty attached great importance. Huang Renyu, a historian, once estimated that it cost 7,700 taels of silver to build one kilometer of the Great Wall in the Ming Dynasty, and up to 31,500 taels of silver was cost. In order to build the Great Wall of the Ming Dynasty with a total length of 6,300 kilometers, it cost at least 48.5 million taels of silver. However, even in the golden period of finance, the annual income of the Ming Dynasty was only 4 million taels of silver. The big investment brought immediate results and the construction of the Great Wall in the Ming Dynasty reached a new peak.

　　西起嘉峪关，东至鸭绿江的长城是明廷最北的防线，设置了都、司、卫、所四级军事组织机构，在北方的山脊间，划出一条与蒙古部族的分界线。

　　The Great Wall, from Jiayu Pass in the west to Yalu River in the east, became the northernmost defense line of the Ming Dynasty. Four-tier military organizations including Regional Military Commissions and Military Settlements were set up. On the ridges in the north, a demarcation line was drawn with the Mongolian tribes.

只是这条戒备森严的防线并未护得京师周全。1449年秋天，明英宗朱祁镇北伐失败，在今张家口境内的土木堡被瓦剌军俘虏，瓦剌军携英宗直逼北京，留下整个明王朝不堪回首的一幕。北京保卫战后，痛定思痛的明廷开始用另一道长墙将京城周围原有的关隘连接起来。1549年，东起居庸关四海冶，西达山西阳高县，全长1023里的次边完工。次边就是内长城，是守卫北京的最后一道防线。

However, this heavily fortified line of defense did not protect the capital. In the autumn of 1449, Zhu Qizhen, Emperor Yingzong of the Ming Dynasty, failed in his northern expedition and was captured by Oriat Mongol army in Tumubu in today's Zhangjiakou. The Oriat Mongols took Emperor Yingzong to Beijing, leaving the whole Ming Dynasty with a scene unbearable to recall. After the Defense of Beijing, the court of the Ming Dynasty, drawing a lesson from the bitter experience, began to connect the existing passes around the capital with another long wall. In 1549, the Secondary Side Wall was completed, with a total length of 1023 li from Sihaiye in Juyong Pass in the east to Yanggao County in Shanxi in the west. This is the Inner Great Wall, the last line of defense for Beijing.

　　明朝把长城沿线划分为九个防区，称为"九边"或者"九镇"，后扩展为"十三镇"。河北境内的明长城分属蓟镇、宣府镇和真保镇，东起秦皇岛山海关老龙头，西至张家口怀安县马市口，南至邯郸武安，全长1338千米。

In the Ming Dynasty, the area along the Great Wall was divided into nine defense areas, which were referred to as "Jiu Bian", also known as "Nine Frontiers" or "Jiu Zhen", knows as "Nine Towns", later the defense areas were expanded to "Thirteen Towns". The Great Wall of the Ming Dynasty in Hebei Province belonged to Ji Town, Xuanfu Town and Zhenbao Town, with a total length of 1338 kilometers from Laolongtou of Shanhai Pass in Qinhuangdao in the east to Mashikou of Huaian County in Zhangjiakou in the west and Wu'an in Handan in the south.

大境门
世界文化遗产

　　古代军事家一直遵循着一项防御原则——因险设塞，以便以较少的兵力抵抗较多的敌人。这一点在明长城的选址上得到完美体现。最大限度地利用山形地势，有的要塞矗立在山巅，锁住峪口；有的隐逸在深谷，封住咽喉。

　　Ancient military strategists always followed a principle of defense, that is, to set up a fortress according to its strategic position, in order to resist more enemies with fewer soldiers. This is perfectly reflected in the site selection of the Great Wall of the Ming Dynasty by making the best use of mountain topography, with some fortresses standing on the top of the mountain to lock the valley pass, and some hiding in the ravine, protecting the country.

这种选择意外地成就了明长城的"长城美学"。长墙城楼与山川地形完美契合，线条绝美。各色建筑与山石植被互为烘托，气势磅礴。"雄、险、奇、长"，即便在岁月中坍塌残缺，长城也有一种壮志难酬的悲壮美。

This kind of choice unexpectedly achieved the "Great Wall aesthetics" of the Great Wall of the Ming Dynasty. Long walls and gate towers perfectly fit the landscape of mountains and rivers with beautiful lines. Various kinds of buildings and rocks and vegetation set off each other with tremendous momentum. "Majestic, dangerous, grotesque and long", the Great Wall is beautiful yet heroic with its noble ambitions unfulfilled even when it collapsed or became incomplete over the past years.

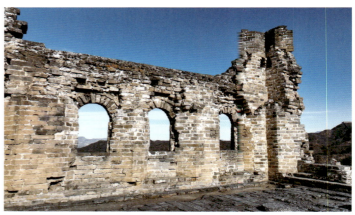

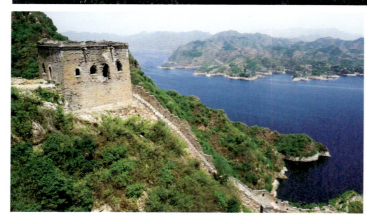

长城之所以伟大，还在于它所拥有的精妙且富有创造性的建筑。边墙与长城这两个称呼，都不能概括它的全部，它是由关隘、城墙、敌楼、烽火台、营城等诸多工事组成的完整防御体系。

What makes the Great Wall great is its ingenious and creative architecture. The two names the Side Wall and the Great Wall cannot sum up all of it, actually it is a complete defense system composed of various fortifications including passes, walls, watchtowers, beacon towers, barracks, etc.

大美河北
世界文化遗产

张家口市怀来县庙港村有一道保存较好的明代长城。民间传说，明朝将领在修筑居庸关长城时，为保证建筑质量，特地在庙港附近的山岭中选择险要地段修建了样板工程，以供修筑长城的人学习。

There is a well-preserved section of the Great Wall of the Ming Dynasty in Miaogang Village, Huailai County of Zhangjiakou. Folklore says that in order to ensure the quality of the construction, when Juyong Pass of the Great Wall was built, the generals in the Ming Dynasty specifically built a model project in the section which is strategically located and difficult to access in the mountain ridge near Miaogang for the builders of the Great Wall to learn.

虽然历经硝烟战火与风雨剥蚀，样边长城仍能看出当时的规制。墙体由石条砌成，城基宽约五米、顶宽约四米、高度在四至八米之间，墙体内侧每两百米设一个门洞、每三百米设敌楼或墙台，城墙上规划有合理的排水装置。明长城的科学性已初见端倪。

Although it has experienced the flames of war and erosion by wind and rain, the size and the structure of the sample project of the Great Wall can still be seen. The wall is made of stone strips, with the wall base of about five meters wide, the top about four meters wide, and the height between four and eight meters. Inside the wall, there was a doorway every two hundred meters, a watchtower or a wall platform every three hundred meters, and reasonable drainage devices were planned on the wall as well. The scientific nature of the Great Wall in the Ming Dynasty had begun to emerge.

1568年，明廷的一个决定，开启了明长城最为辉煌的一页。这年春天，戚继光调任蓟镇总兵，管辖蓟镇境内的1500余里长城。在随后的十六年间，战神戚继光以长城设计师的新身份翻修改造出明长城最精华的一段。

　　In 1568, a decision by the Government of the Ming Dynasty opened the most glorious page of the Great Wall of the Ming Dynasty. In this spring, Qi Jiguang was transferred to be the Commanding Officer of Ji Town, having jurisdiction over more than 1,500 li of the Great Wall in Ji Town. During the next 16 years, Qi Jiguang, the God of War, rebuilt the best part of the Great Wall in the Ming Dynasty in his new identity as the designer of the Great Wall.

　　给旧长城包上青砖，是戚继光的一大创举。砖包墙的工艺，并未改变长城的形态，却让它的坚固性提升。

　　It was a pioneering work of Qi Jiguang to cover the old Great Wall with black bricks, which did not change the shape of the Great Wall, but made it sturdier.

在秦皇岛板厂峪，有两百多座砖窑遗迹。当年戚继光率义乌兵北上，在这里开窑烧砖，以供修筑长城之用，主要烧制长形城砖、方形漫地砖、瓦等建筑构件。

In Banchangyu of Qinhuangdao, there are ruins of more than 200 brick kilns. When Qi Jiguang led soldiers from Yiwu of Zhejiang to the north, they set up kilns to bake bricks for the building of the Great Wall, mainly firing long city wall bricks, square floor tiles, tiles and other architectural components.

戚继光将他的代表作，经浙江台州试验行之有效的空心敌楼，在金山岭发扬光大，走向极致。全长10.5千米的金山岭设有空心敌楼67座，最远间隔200多米，最近的不足50米，是明长城中空心敌楼最为密集多样的一段。一旦迎敌，相望相助，构成一道严密的防御体系。

Qi Jiguang carried forward in Jinshanling his masterpiece, the hollow watchtower, which was tested and proved to be effective in Taizhou of Zhejiang Province. With a total length of 10.5 kilometers, there are 67 hollow watchtowers on Jinshanling. With the longest interval of more than 200 meters and the shortest of less than 50 meters, it is a section of the most dense and diverse hollow watchtowers. In case there was enemy, they could see and help each other, thus making up a strict defense system.

金山岭的名称来自两座名为大小金山的高峰。据说，来自江浙的士兵负责修建这两座山岭上的长城，他们将家乡金山岛的名字借用到这里，以解乡愁。

Jinshanling gets its name from two peaks known as Big Jinshan and Small Jinshan. It is said that soldiers from Jiangsu and Zhejiang Provinces were responsible for the construction of the Great Wall on the two ridges, and they borrowed the name of their hometown Jinshan Island here to relieve their homesickness.

小金山楼是一座典型的三层空心敌楼，入口极为隐秘。宽大的基座之上是券室，供守台士兵居住和储存物资，由一道隐秘的石梯与上层连接。上层台顶有供放哨的望亭，四周垛口墙开设射孔，中间建铺房以供将士休息。

Small Jinshan Tower is a typical three-storeyed hollow watchtower, with a very secret entrance. On the large base, there are arched rooms for the guards to live in and store supplies, which are connected to the upper floors by a hidden stone staircase. On the top of the platform there is a lookout pavilion for sentry, in the surrounding crenel walls there are perforations, and in the middle there are rooms for soldiers to rest.

　　将军楼是金山岭防御体系的指挥中枢，楼两侧的烽火台传递军情。北侧从长城主线延伸而出的支墙，便于兵力运动。挡马墙、月墙抵挡敌人骑兵。前后马道布有密集的障墙，可作为掩体阻击攻上长城的敌人。南侧建有一座战时指挥所，这在明长城上难得一见。

The General Tower was the command center of Jinshanling defense system, and the beacon towers on both sides of the building conveyed military messages. The bracing wall extending from the main line of the Great Wall in the north facilitated the movement of troops. The horse-blocking wall and the moon-shaped wall held off the enemy cavalry. In the front and the back of the bridle path there were dense barrier walls, which could be used as shelters to block the enemy attacking on the Great Wall. On the south side, there was built a wartime command post, which was rarely seen on the Great Wall of the Ming Dynasty.

麒麟楼得名于楼顶上的"麒麟影壁"。影壁由十五块浮雕着麒麟的长城方砖组成,这是万里长城中唯一的一座。麒麟,在中国文化中是吉祥的象征。这座麒麟影壁并无实用功能,更多地寄托着筑城将士的希望,祈求和平与安宁。

Kylin Tower got its name from the "Kylin Screen Wall" on the roof. The only screen wall in the Great Wall consisted of 15 square bricks of the Great Wall decorated in relief with Kylin. Kylin was a symbol of auspiciousness in Chinese culture. This kylin screen wall had no practical functions, but the soldiers who built the wall placed their hopes on it, praying for peace and tranquility.

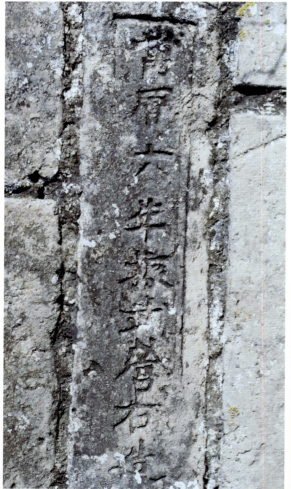

金山岭上还有一段600米的墙体与众不同，大约有七成由带有文字的青砖砌成。主要文字有"万历五年镇虏奇兵营造""万历六年振武营右造"等七种。据考证，文字砖记录的是修建长城的年代和部队番号，用于工程质量的追责。或许这也是这段长城历经四百多年变迁，仍然屹立在山巅的缘故。

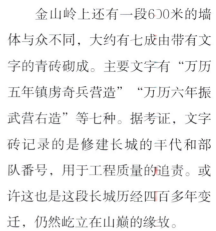

There is also a section of wall about 600 meters long in Jinshanling which is different from the rest. About 70 percent of this section is made of black bricks with characters. There are mainly seven texts including "built by Zhenlu Battalion for ingenious military moves in the fifth year of Wanli" and "built by the right-wing forces of Zhenwu Battalion in the sixth year of Wanli". According to textual research, the texted bricks record the time and the designation of the troops who built the Great Wall, for accountability of the project quality. Perhaps this is the reason why this section of the Great Wall still stood on the top of the mountain after more than 400 years of changes.

与外长城的壮观相比，明代内长城既朴实又低调。内长城关隘多设在太行山地区，太行八陉的军都陉，又称居庸陉，设有居庸关。稍南的飞狐陉、蒲阴陉，设有倒马关和紫荆关，这便是史书上著名的"内三关"。

　　Compared with the grandeur of the Outer Wall, the Inner Wall of the Ming Dynasty was rather simple and kept a low profile. The passes on the Inner Great Wall were mostly located in Taihang Mountains. Jundu Xing (Xing means mountain pass) was one of the eight passes in Taihang Mountains, also known as Juyong Xing, where was set Juyong Pass. Daoma Pass and Zijing Pass were set in Feihu Xing and Puyin Xing, a little south to Juyong Xing. They were known as the "Three Inner Passes" in historical books.

乌龙沟长城地处倒马关与紫荆关之间，这一段的长城广设敌楼，10千米的长城上设置七十一座敌楼。工事密布，普通的山川也就成了天险。

　　The Great Wall at Wulonggou was located between Daoma Pass and Zijing Pass, and watchtowers were widely set up on this section. There were 71 watchtowers on its ten-kilometer wall. With fortifications densely built, the ordinary mountains and rivers here became natural defense.

大境门
世界文化遗产

内长城多就地取材，以太行山特有的红砂岩为原材料，墙体多为石砌，随着山势，与险隘、深壑融合。邢台市境内的鹤度岭长城，墙体就是毛石巧垒的花墙，明代的巧匠不仅能利用这些大小各异的石头砌墙，还能把起伏转弯的石墙立面拼接得平整如一。支锅岭长城为碎石墙，防御功能并不突出，最主要的是标划地界。

The Inner Great Wall was mostly built with local materials. The red sandstone unique in the Taihang Mountains was used as raw materials. The wall was mostly built of stone, extending along the mountain ridges and integrating into the narrow passes and deep valleys. The Great Wall of Heduling in Xingtai City was characterized by its wall of rough stone latticework. Craftsmen in the Ming Dynasty could not only build walls with stones of different sizes, but also pieced together the stones on the façade of undulating and turning walls flat and even. The Great Wall of Zhiguoling was the crushed stone wall, which did not have outstanding defense functions, but mainly demarcated borders.

在辽西走廊的最西端，渤海与角山构成天然屏障，山海之间只有8千米，咽喉锁钥，自古就是华北通往东北的要冲。这里距北京280千米，两地之间多是利于骑兵冲杀的平原，它的存亡关乎京师安危。明初在此设立卫所，从明朝中后期开始，雄踞此地的山海关逐渐赢得了"天下第一关"的称号。

At the westernmost end of the Liaoxi Corridor, the Bohai Sea and Jiaoshan Mountain formed a natural barrier. There were only eight kilometers between the mountain and the sea. As a vital passage, it had been the strategic point from North China to Northeast China since ancient times. It was 280 kilometers away from Beijing, and the plain between the two places was conducive for cavalry to charge. Its survival was related to the safety of the capital. In the early Ming Dynasty, Military Settlements were set up here. From the middle and late Ming Dynasty, Shanhaiguan Pass, which was magnificently situated here, gradually won the title of "the First Pass under Heaven".

长城
The Great Wall | **47**

能称"天下第一关",山海关自有其气势,山海关城几乎囊括了中国古代所有先进的城防建筑体系。关城的两侧一千多米的长城线上,靖边楼、牧营楼、镇东楼、临闾楼和威远堂依次排开,五虎镇东。城外四瓮城拱卫,外层筑有罗城、翼城、卫城、哨城,壁垒森严。瓮城另有乾坤,如遇敌人侵扰,可将关门作为二道防线,制敌如瓮中捉鳖。

Shanhaiguan Pass could be called the First Pass under Heaven, as it has its own momentum. It contained almost all the advanced city defense building systems in ancient China. On both sides of the pass city, along the Great Wall of more than 1,000 meters long, Jingbian Tower, Muying Tower, Zhendong Tower, Linlv Tower and Weiyuan Hall lined up in turn, like five tigers guarding the east. There were four enclosures for defense outside the city gate. In the outer layer, there were the Outer City, the Wing City, the Citadel, and the Sentry City was built independently from the main wall, which were all closely guarded. In the enclosures outside the city gate, there was another implication. In case of enemy intrusion, the gate of the Pass City could be used as a second line of defense to control the enemy like catching a turtle in a jar.

可惜历史从来不按常理出牌。1644年4月，多尔衮率领十五万清军直扑长城九门口，吴三桂打开山海关城门迎敌入关，这座固若金汤的关城没来得及发挥自己的防御威力。

Unfortunately, history never plays by the rules. In April 1644, Dorgon led 150,000 troops of the Qing Dynasty to attack Jiumenkou of the Great Wall. Wu Sangui opened the gate of Shanhaiguan Pass to meet the enemy. The impregnable city did not have time to give play to its defensive power.

长城，虽然以防御姿态出现，但在世人眼里更多的却是一种象征。明代的有识之士曾经说："重关叠嶂，险在地者也；谋臣猛士，险在人者也；懔懔危惧，险在心者也。"对于一个国家来说，险关要塞不可或缺，但众志成城、不屈不挠更为重要。

Although the Great Wall appeared in a defensive posture, it was more of a symbol in the eyes of the world. A man of insight in the Ming Dynasty once said, "Danger lies in the land where the mountains rise one after another. Danger lies in the people where the councilors and warriors are. Danger and fear lie in the heart." For a country, the perilous and strategic passes and fortresses are indispensable, but unity and perseverance are more important.

这是长城所独有的坚强意志和伟大力量，这种意志与力量曾拯救中华民族于水火之中。当帝国主义入侵中华之际，"把我们的血肉筑成我们新的长城"，凝聚起了全民族救亡图存的决心与必胜的力量。

This is the unique strong will and great strength of the Great Wall, which has saved the Chinese nation from an abyss of misery. When the imperialists invaded China, "building our flesh and blood into our new Great Wall" gathered the determination of the whole nation to save their country so that it may survive and the strength to win.

虽名为城，与城市的城墙相比，长城的姿态更为开放。在大多数岁月里，成千上万的关口不是为了阻拦，而是为了交流。长城构建了长城内外的交流秩序。

Although it was called a "城" (city), the Great Wall was more open than the walls of cities. In most years, thousands of passes were not for obstruction, but for communication. The Great Wall constructed the communication order inside and outside the Great Wall.

从秦代开始，沿着长城移民实边，屯田制度让长城两边人口数量增加。尽管生活方式不同，可即便是在对立时期，两边民族互通有无的举动从未止息。以防御为初衷建起的长城，在更为广阔的空间里，却以民族间贸易与融合平台的形象示人。

Since the Qin Dynasty, people had migrated along the Great Wall, and the settlement system of garrison troops or peasants opening up wasteland and growing food grain increased the population on both sides of the Great Wall. Despite the different ways of life, even in the period of confrontation, the exchange of needs between the two ethnic groups never stopped. The Great Wall which was built with the original intention of defense showed itself as a platform for inter-ethnic trade and integration in a broader space.

大境门，意为边境之门，这是长城关口中唯一被称为门的地方。关，关门闭户的关；门，开门迎客的门，一字之差道尽长城内外的交流与融合。

Dajingmen which means the gate of the border was the only place that was called a gate in all the passes on the Great Wall. Pass, means "close" in "close the gate" in Chinese; gate, means "opening the gate" to welcome guests. The difference of one word expresses the communication and integration inside and outside the Great Wall.

张家口城外的元宝山一直是边境贸易的市场，古称"贡市"或者"茶马互市"，来自蒙古草原和欧洲腹地的牲畜、皮毛等货物在此处换成丝绸、茶叶。封建王朝以长城为界，做生意的外族人只能在长城外交易。

Yuanbaoshan outside Zhangjiakou was always a market for border trade, which was known as "Gongshi" where foreign or alien merchants accompanied tributary envoys to designated places for trade, or "Tea-horse and Trade Market" where livestock, fur and other goods from the Mongolian steppe and the hinterland of Europe were exchanged for silk and tea. The feudal dynasties took the Great Wall as the boundary, and the foreigners who did business could only trade outside the Great Wall.

大好河北
世界文化遗产

1644年，随着贸易规模不断扩大，长城开豁建门，大境门就此面世。此后，与"丝绸之路"相媲美的古商道"张库大道"从这里出发，通往蒙古草原腹地，并延伸至俄罗斯。

In 1644, with the continuous expansion of the scale of trade, the Great Wall was opened and Dajingmen was built. It is from here that "Zhangjiakou-Khuree Routes", an ancient trade route which could be compared with the "Silk Road" had started since then, leading to the hinterland of Mongolian steppe and extending to Russia.

如今的长城，以一种更为开放的姿态面对世界。在大境门北边的崇礼，古老的长城正在邂逅一场国际盛会，在长城的怀抱中，激情飞扬，冰雪相约，历史与现代交汇，中国与世界共舞。夜色中，被灯火点亮的长城闪耀于崇礼群山之间，长城牵手五环，成为冬奥盛会中最醒目的背景，向全世界传递着热情的问候。

Today, the Great Wall faces the world with a more open attitude. In Chongli, north of Dajingmen, the ancient Great Wall is meeting an international event. In the embrace of the Great Wall, passion flies, ice meets snow, history meets modernity, and China dances with the world. In the dim light of night, the Great Wall is lit up with lights, shining in the mountains of Chongli. The Great Wall, holding hands with the five rings, becomes the most eye-catching background of the Winter Olympic Games and conveys warm greetings to the whole world.

　　在这里，聚焦全球目光的崇礼桦岭东长城是中国正在建设中的长城国家文化公园的一部分。而在更广阔的远方，老龙头、大境门、金山岭长城也都加入了长城传承保护利用示范样板工程。未来，这种保护利用新模式将覆盖河北境内的所有长城，传承与守护并行，景观与文化齐飞。长城国家文化公园将成为彰显中华优秀传统文化持久影响力、社会主义先进文化强大生命力的重要文化地标。长城区域的经济发展也因长城国家文化公园的建设而焕发新的生机与活力，生活在长城两边的人们也迎来了一个更值得期待的前景。

Here, the Great Wall of Hualingdong in Chongli, which focuses the world attention, is part of the Great Wall National Cultural Park under construction in China. In the broader distance, Laolongtou, Dajingmen and Jinshanling Great Wall have also joined the Demonstration Model Project of Inheritance, Protection and Utilization of the Great Wall. In the future, this new mode of protection and utilization will cover all the Great Wall in Hebei Province, with inheritance and protection going hand in hand, and landscape and culture developing together. The Great Wall National Cultural Park will become an important cultural landmark to highlight the lasting influence of Chinese excellent traditional culture and the strong vitality of advanced socialist culture. The economic development of the Great Wall region has also been revitalized by the construction of the Great Wall National Cultural Park, and people living on both sides of the Great Wall have also ushered in a more promising future.

　　雄关漫道真如铁，而今迈步从头越。"上下两千年，纵横十万里"的长城，早已凭借其视觉冲击与精神震撼，成为国家记忆不可或缺的一部分。它是史诗，也是图腾，是国人一生必须到过一次的集体向往。从最早的防御工事，到后来民族融合的纽带，再到今天的国家文化公园，长城，它的未来将与过去一样漫长。不管身份如何变换，"长城"这个名称唤起的永远是中华民族共同的意志与情感。

The strong pass is like a wall of iron, yet with firm strides, we are conquering its summit. With "two thousand years of history and tens of thousands miles of territory", the Great Wall has already become an indispensable part of the national memories by virtue of its visual impact and spiritual shock. It is an epic, a totem, and a collective yearning that Chinese people must realize once in their lives. From the earliest fortifications, to the later ties of national integration, to today's national cultural park, the future of the Great Wall will be as long as its past. No matter how the identity changes, the name of the "Great Wall" shall always evoke the common will and emotion of the Chinese nation.

2

North of the Great River: World Cultural Heritage

Chengde Mountain Resort

避暑山庄

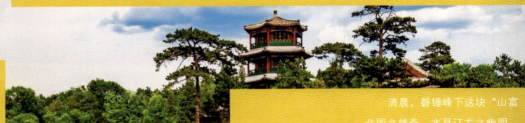

清晨，磬锤峰下这块"山富北国之雄奇，水具江左之幽明，呈南北郁结而兼美"的宝地，开始苏醒。

公元1703年，康熙帝开始设计和指挥行宫的建造。他无比看重这个自己立意创建的园林。北京的紫禁城和颐和园都是继承自前代，而在这里，他可以实现自己包容天下的雄心。这时的康熙帝，已经取得了政治与军事的胜利，收获了经济、科技和文化的辉煌，他把对未来"万世缔构"的自信充分地释放在这片美景之中。

在河北最北端，与内蒙古交界的地方，有一片全球最大的人工林海，这就是塞罕坝。

In the northernmost part of Hebei Province, near the border with Inner Mongolia, there lies Saihanba, the world's largest sea of artificial forest.

　　三百多年前，这里曾是清代康熙帝圈定的木兰围场。每年秋天，康熙帝亲率大军，与北方的蒙古王公一同狩猎，史称"木兰秋狝"。驰骋比武、分旗封王、经济援助，数万骁勇善战的将士逐鹿草原，这既是一年一度的军事演习，也是清王朝与北方民族结盟的盛会。

More than three hundred years ago, here it used to be the Mulan Paddock delineated by Emperor Kangxi of the Qing Dynasty. Every autumn, Emperor Kangxi personally led a huge army to hunt with the Mongolian lords in the north, which is known as "Mulan Autumn Hunting" in history. Tens of thousands of brave and skillful soldiers galloped in the steppe, competing in military skills, for enfeoffment and economic assistance. It was not only an annual military exercise, but also a grand gathering for the Qing Dynasty to ally with the northern nationalities.

　　"木兰秋狝"可谓是康熙帝巩固统一大业的一大谋略。而为了让这道塞上雄藩永固百年，康熙帝谋划了一个更为庞大的体系，秋狝的必经之地热河，纳入了他的视野。

"Mulan Autumn Hunting" was a great strategy for Emperor Kangxi to consolidate the great cause of unification. He planned a larger system in order to make this powerful state on the north of the Great Wall last hundreds of years. Rehe, which must be passed through in the autumn hunting, came into his view.

热河，位于从北方高原进入中原大地的一条要道上，它距北京约200千米，"朝发夕至，往还无过两日"。在热河建造一座行宫，向东可连通东北，向北可沟通蒙古，向西北可联络蒙回各部，向南可控制中原。

Rehe, located on a main road from the northern plateau to the Central Plains, is about 200 kilometers away from Beijing. "Starting at dawn and arriving at dusk, it is a journey of less than two days". If a palace was built in Rehe, it could connect the northeast to the east, link Mongolia on the north, contact the tribes of Mongolia and Hui in the northwest, and control the Central Plains in the south.

于是，建避暑山庄，修外八庙，在热河，帝王宫苑与皇家寺庙相辉映，开创了民族团结与文化交融的典范。

Therefore, Chengde Mountain Resort was built and Eight Outer Temples were constructed. In Rehe, the imperial palace and the royal temples reflected one another, creating a model of national unity and cultural integration.

清晨，磬锤峰下这块"山富北国之雄奇，水具江左之幽明，呈南北郁结而兼美"的宝地，开始苏醒。

Early in the morning, at the foot of the Hammer Peak, the treasure land begins to wake up, where "the mountain has the magnificence of the north, and the water has the seclusion and brightness of the south, showing both the melancholy and beauty from south to north".

公元1703年，康熙帝开始设计和指挥行宫的建造。他无比看重这个自己立意创建的园林。北京的紫禁城和颐和园都是继承自前代，而在这里，他可以实现自己包容天下的雄心。这时的康熙帝，已经取得了政治与军事的胜利，收获了经济、科技和文化的辉煌，他把对未来"万世缔构"的自信充分地释放在这片美景之中。

In 1703, Emperor Kangxi began to design and direct the construction of the palace. He attached great importance to this garden he had decided to create. The Forbidden City and the Summer Palace in Beijing were inherited from previous generations, and here he could fulfill his ambition to embrace the world. At this time, Emperor Kangxi had won political and military victories, and reaped brilliant achievements of economy, science and technology and culture. He fully released his confidence in the future "eternal construction" in this beautiful landscape.

大承德 世界文化遗产

五年后，行宫初步建成。总面积5.64平方公里的避暑山庄，分为宫殿区、湖区、平原区、山区四个部分。从西北部最高峰到东南部湖沼、平湖地带，相对等差180米，整体上就表现出一种四方朝揖、众向所归的气势。西北部的巍巍群山仿佛北部的边疆，中部的万树园好比是蒙古草原和东北森林的混合体，东部的楼阁亭榭极具江南韵味，高低起伏的宫墙蜿蜒在北部的山岭之上，酷似中国北部疆土上雄伟的长城。这一切正好像是整个中国版图的缩影。"北控远烟息，南临近毼嘉"，康熙帝的诗句将避暑山庄对内对外的军事、政治意义表达得透彻而又自得。

　　Five years later, the palace was initially completed. With a total area of 5. 64 square kilometers, Chengde Mountain Resort was divided into four parts: the Palace Area, the Lake Area, the P1ain Area and the Mountain Area. From the highest peak in the northwest to the lakes and marshes and flat lake area in the southeast, the relative equal difference is 180 meters, which shows a kind of momentum of bowing and returning from all directions. The lofty mountains in the northwest are like the northern frontier; Wanshu Yuan (Garden of Ten Thousand Trees) in the middle is like a mixture of the Mongolian steppe and the forest in the northeast; the pavilions and towers in the east are full of charm of the regions south of the Yangtze River, and the undulating palace walls are winding on the mountain ridges in the north, just like the magnificent Great Wall in northern China. All this seems to be a microcosm of the whole territory of China. "In the north the situation is controlled and the flames of war have subsided, while in the south the beautiful scenery of the mountains makes people happy". Emperor Kangxi's poem expresses the internal and external military and political significance of Chengde Mountain Resort thoroughly and complacently.

大承德
世界文化遗产

海上生明月，九州共此时。远在欧洲的旷世哲人黑格尔察觉到了这位亚洲皇帝的用心：通过避暑山庄清王朝降低了政治姿态，巩固了与蒙藏高层的关系，拉近了与藩属国的相互情感，间接实现了清朝皇帝安抚、团结中国边疆少数民族，巩固国家统一的政治目的。

The bright moon rises above the sea; everyone faraway enjoys the same moment. Hegel, a great philosopher in Europe, perceived the intention of the Asian emperor: through Chengde Mountain Resort, the Qing Dynasty kept a low profile in politics, consolidated the high-level relations with Mongolia and Tibet, drew closer the mutual feelings with the Vassal States, and indirectly achieved the political purpose of the Emperor of the Qing Dynasty to appease and unite China's frontier minorities and consolidate national unity.

　　而这一切的一切，都是由一汪清泉开始。据说，最早康熙帝看重这块土地，就是因为这里有一汪清泉，因泉水水温常年保持8℃左右，故而名为"热河"。每到冬季，水面上霞光瑞彩，云雾蒸腾，富于变化。有时水雾摇曳着身姿，以水龙卷的样式向天空升起，成为冬日热河的胜景。

　　All of this began with a clear spring or fountain. It is said that Emperor Kangxi first valued this land only because there was a clear spring here. Its water temperature was at about 8℃ all the year round, thus got the name Rehe, literally meaning "hot river". In winter, the water glistens with rays of sunlight, clouds and mists slowly rising, full of changes. Sometimes the water spray sways and rises into the sky like a waterspout, becoming a scenic beauty of Rehe in winter.

雍正帝即位后，取"承受先祖德泽"之意，将"热河"改为"承德"，而他的继任者乾隆帝，又在康熙帝布局避暑山庄的基础之上，移南方胜境入北园，使避暑山庄有了"南秀北雄"的兼美之意，精彩之处也从三十六景翻倍为七十二景。

After Emperor Yongzheng ascended to the throne, he changed "Rehe" to "Chengde", taking the meaning of "bearing the ancestor's kindness and benevolence". While his successor Emperor Qianlong, on the basis of Emperor Kangxi's layout of Chengde Mountain Resort, moved the scenic spots of the south into the garden in the north, thus Chengde Mountain Resort took both "the grace of the south and grandeur of the north of China", and doubled its scenic sites from 36 to 72.

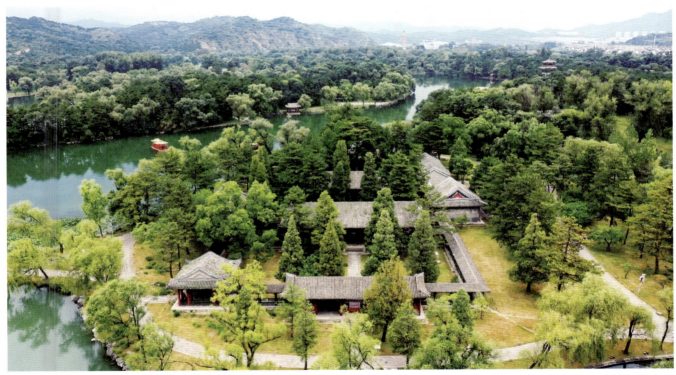

康熙与乾隆乐此不疲参与建筑设计，将他们的襟怀、审美趣味深深地倾注到这座皇家园林。世间一切好物，皆为此所用，"移天缩地在君怀"，避暑山庄集中国古代造园艺术和建筑艺术之大成于一身。

Emperor Kangxi and Qianlong were never tired of participating in architectural design and deeply poured their minds and aesthetic interests into this imperial garden. All the good things in the world are used for this purpose. "Moving the sky and shrinking the earth in their arms", Chengde Mountain Resort is a combination of ancient Chinese arts of gardening and architecture.

避暑山庄最核心的区域是正宫，由九进院落组成。与紫禁城一样，它遵守"前朝后寝"的形制，中轴对称、院落重门的严整格局并未改变。只是宫殿顶上不用琉璃瓦，不起飞脊，木柱古朴，青砖灰瓦，不饰彩绘，有一种北方民居的风格。与紫禁城巍峨华贵的宫殿相比，带着文人审美意趣的山庄宫殿更为雅致亲民。

The core area of Chengde Mountain Resort was the Main Palace, which was composed of nine courtyards. Like the Forbidden City, it followed the structure of "court in the front and living quarters at the rear", and the strict pattern of symmetrical central axis and several parallel doors in courtyards has not changed. But on the roof of the palace, there were no glazed tiles and no extremly high ridges, and the wooden pillars were of primitive simplicity, there were black bricks and grey tiles, and no painted decorations, all of which exhibiting a style of northern civilian residence. Compared with the magnificent palaces in the Forbidden City, those in Chengde Mountain Resort with aesthetic taste of the literati were more elegant and close to the people.

丽正门是山庄的大门，名称取自《易经》"日月丽于天"，意为光明正大的门。门额采用满、藏、汉、维、蒙五种文字书写，多民族大一统的意味不言而喻。

Lizhengmen (Gate of Righteousness), was the main gate of Chengde Mountain Resort, which was named from "Sun and Moon are clinging in the sky" in *Book of Changes*, meaning righteous and aboveboard gate. At the top part of the lintel it was written in the five languages of Manchu, Tibetan, Han, Uygur and Mongolian, and the meaning of multi-ethnic unification was self-evident.

沿着丽正门这条中轴线，青砖甬道依次串联起阅射门、淡泊敬诚殿、四知书屋、烟波致爽殿、云山胜地楼等建筑，皇帝的日常生活、王朝的波澜壮阔，都在这条线上一一上演。

Along the central axis of Lizhengmen, the black brick corridor linked up such buildings as Yueshemen (Gate for Reviewing the Archers), Danbo Jingcheng (Hall of Simplicity and Piety), Sizhi Shuwu (Study of Four "Knows"), Yanbo Zhishuang (Hall of Refreshing Mists and Waves) and Yunshan Shengdi (House of Cloudy Mountains) in turn. The daily life of the Emperors and the magnificence of the Dynasty were all staged on this line.

阅射门，顾名思义，是皇帝接见臣属、举行射箭比赛的地方，门上悬有康熙亲题的"避暑山庄"匾额。

Yueshemen (Gate for Reviewing the Archers), as its name implied, was the place where the emperor receives his vassals and held archery competitions. On the door hung a horizontal board with the inscription of "Summer Resort" written by Kangxi himself.

在阅射门后静默的是山庄正殿澹泊敬诚殿。"澹泊"二字源于《易经》中的"不烦不扰，澹泊不失"。虽外表色彩素雅，殿内陈设简洁，但面阔七楹、进深五间的结构，金丝楠木的质地，仍显示出不凡的气质。事实上，它地位超然，等同于紫禁城的太和殿，是举行重大庆典、处理公务、接见少数民族首领和外国使节的地方。

Danbo Jingcheng (Hall of Simplicity and Piety), the Main Hall of Chengde Mountain Resort, stands silently behind Yueshemen. The word "Dan Bo" originated from *Book of Changes*, which means "no bother, no disturbance, seeking no fame and wealth and no loss". Although the exterior color is simple but elegant and the furnishings in the hall are simple, the structure of seven principle columns wide and five rooms deep, and the texture of phoebe zhennan wood still show extraordinary temperament. In fact, it is incomparably superior and equivalent to the Hall of Supreme Harmony in the Forbidden City. It is the place where important celebrations were held, official business was handled, and ethnic minority leaders and foreign envoys were received.

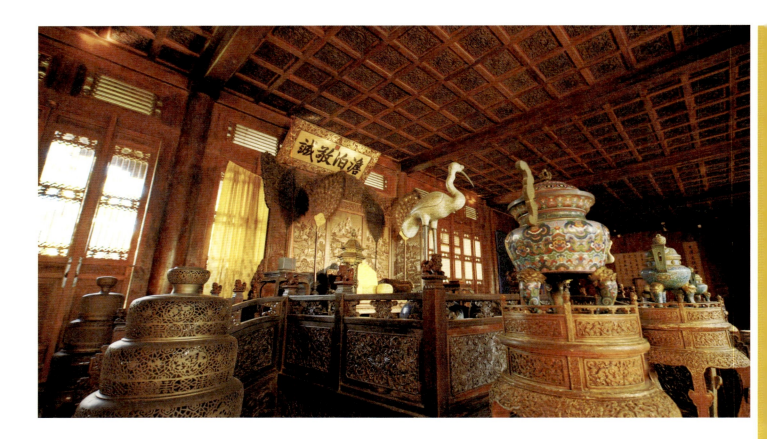

　　1771年9月18日，澹泊敬诚殿上演了清代历史上最有张力、最为难忘的一幕，乾隆帝接见了万里东归的土尔扈特部杰出领袖渥巴锡一行。游牧在伏尔加河流域的土尔扈特部原本是中国蒙古族中一个古老的部落。1771年1月5日，因不堪沙俄的控制与奴役，在首领渥巴锡的带领下，土尔扈特部回归中国。他们一路突破沙俄、哥萨克和哈萨克等军队的不断围追堵截，战胜了难以想象的艰难困苦，出发时尚有17万人口，"其至伊犁者，仅以半计"。

On September 18, 1771, the most dramatic and unforgettable scene in the history of the Qing Dynasty was staged in Danbo Jingcheng. Emperor Qianlong received Ubashi Khan, an outstanding leader of the Turghut tribe who had returned thousands of miles to the east. Turghut tribe, nomadic in the Volga River Basin, was originally an ancient tribe of Mongolians in China. On January 5, 1771, under the leadership of Ubashi Khan, the Turghut tribe returned to China because they could not bear the control and slavery of Tsarist Russia. Along the way, they broke through constant encirclement, pursuit, obstruction and interception of the armies of Tsarist Russia, Cossack, and Kazakh, and overcame unimaginable difficulties and hardships. They set out with a population of 170,000, but "only half of them arrived in Ili".

　　土尔扈特部对祖国的强烈认同，得到祖国的热烈回应，在澹泊敬诚殿，乾隆帝代表清廷给予他们一系列的封赏。

　　The strong recognition of motherland of the Turghut tribe received a warm response from the motherland, and Emperor Qianlong, on behalf of the Government of the Qing Dynasty, granted them a series of awards in Danbo Jingcheng.

　　封赏过后，乾隆帝又在澹泊敬诚殿北边的四知书屋召见渥巴锡，听他面诉土尔扈特部悲壮的东返过程和祖辈的光荣历史。

　　After granting the award, Emperor Qianlong called in Ubashi Khan at Sizhi Shuwu on the north of Danbo Jingcheng, and listened to him tell about the heroic and stirring process of the Turghut tribe's return to the east and the glorious history of their ancestors.

四知书屋的名称同样来自《易经》，取"君子知微、知彰、知柔、知刚，万夫之望"之意。虽说顶着"书屋"的名称，却并不只是读书的地方，而是皇帝临朝前后更衣小憩、接见近臣和贵客的便殿。

The name of Sizhi Shuwu (Study of the Four "Knows"), also comes from Book of Changes, which means "those who know the subtle signs and also the manifest signs of things, the weak side and also the firm side of things are admired by all". Although it bears the name "Study", it is not only a place for reading, but also a temporary hall for the Emperor to change clothes and take a rest before and after the court, and to receive close ministers and distinguished guests.

　　当年的风云变幻已经远去，四知书屋存留陈设依稀可见昔日的风华。紫檀雕花宝座床、紫檀宝座体现着主人的身份，乾隆帝与嘉庆帝的手书贴落字迹依然清晰。屋内的各色陈设品相不凡，西间炕上的十二扇漆地描金点翠玻璃围屏，由名臣刘墉题诗、画家金廷标作画。

The vicissitudes of those days have gone away and the remaining furnishings of Sizhi Shuwu still show the elegance of the past. Red sandalwood-carved throne-bed and red sandalwood throne reflect the identity of the master, and the handwriting of Emperor Qianlong and Emperor Jiaqing is still clear. All kinds of furnishings in the house are extraordinary. On the Kang (a heatable brick bed in north China) in the west room, there are twelve glass folding screens on lacquer ground with gold tracing and kingfisher craft, on which Liu Yong a famous minister, inscribed a poem, and Jin Tingbiao a painter drew a picture.

宫殿之间，广植树木，苍松成行，虬枝如盖。在参天古木之间，些许小精灵流连其间，它们世居于此，穿梭于高大的青松与深幽的宫闱之间，想必它们的祖先也是以这样的状态与当年的清帝及宫人们相处的。

Between the palaces, trees are widely planted. The green pines are in rows, and the branches are like a cover. Some little creatures are lingering on the towering ancient trees. They have lived here for generations, shuttling between the tall pine trees and the deep palaces. Their ancestors must have been in such a state to get along with the emperors of the Qing Dynasty and the imperial concubines or the palace servants.

四知书屋往北是皇帝的寝宫庭院，主殿烟波致爽殿是皇帝的寝宫。主殿东西两侧各有一个小跨院，为后、妃居住之所。

To the north of Sizhi Shuwu was the Emperor's bedroom courtyard, and the main hall Yanbo Zhishuang (Hall of Refreshing Mists and Waves), was the sleeping quarter of the Emperor. There was a small courtyard on the east and west sides of the main hall each, where the empresses and concubines live.

1860年，英法联军入侵北京，离京避难的咸丰帝暂居于此。也正是在这里，咸丰批准了《北京条约》，致使香港与祖国分离长达百年之久。

In 1860, the Anglo-French Allied Forces invaded Beijing, Emperor Xianfeng left Beijing and took refuge here temporarily. It was also here that Emperor Xianfeng ratified the Convention of Peking, which separated Hong Kong from its motherland for a hundred years.

一年之后，回京无望的咸丰帝在烟波致爽殿中走完了自己的人生之路。居住在西边跨院的慈禧与恭亲王奕䜣商定了回北京发动政变的计划。慈禧就此登上了清王朝的政治舞台，垂帘听政，开始她长达48年的统治。

　　A year later, Emperor Xianfeng, who had no hope of returning to Beijing, passed away in Yanbo Zhishuang. Cixi, whc lived in the west courtyard, and the Grand Prince Yixin agreed on a plan of returning to Beijing to launch a coup. Cixi, the Empress Dowager, thus began to attend court affairs behind the screen, stepped onto the political stage of the Qing Dynasty and began her 48-year reign.

正宫的最后一幢建筑是云山胜地楼，楼上为皇帝礼佛诵经之所，虽为楼却未建楼梯，楼前由岩石堆砌而成的祥云状石阶，是皇帝步入佛国时的云山之路。

The last building of the Main Palace was Yunshan Shengdi（House of Cloudy Mountains）. The upper floor was the place where the emperor worshipped Buddha and chanted sutras. Although it was a storied building, there was no staircase. The steps made of rocks in the shape of auspicious clouds in front of the building were the way of cloudy mountains when the emperor entered the Buddhist kingdom.

高大的建筑往往坐落在敦厚的台基之上。木结构的建筑易损，夯土砌石而成的台基，成为最恒久、最有生命力的部分。正是因为有了台基，今天我们才得以在侵华日军和火灾的接连侵蚀后窥见东宫这组建筑群的庞大与恢宏。东宫，顾名思义，位于正宫之东，虽然前殿、清音阁、福寿园、勤政殿都已不复存在，但所幸它的最后一层，名为"卷阿胜境"的建筑仍伫立于塞湖之滨。《卷阿》是《诗经》中的一首颂美诗，赞颂的是雍容祥和的盛世气象，或许正是这个名字才注定了它不会轻易残损的命运。

Tall buildings are often located on solid platforms. The wooden structure of the building is vulnerable, and the platform base made of rammed earth masonry has become the most permanent and vital part. It is precisely because of the platform that today we can see the hugeness and magnificence of the buildings in the East Palace after the Japanese invasion and fires. The East Palace, as its name implies, is located on the east of the Main Palace. Although the Front Hall, Qingyin Ge (Pavilion of Clear Sound), Fushou Yuan (Garden of Happiness and Longevity) and Qinzheng Dian (Hall of Diligence in State Affairs) no longer exist, but fortunately, in the last row, the building named "Quane Shengjing" (Hall of Celebrate Splendors), still stands on the shore of Saihu Lake. "Quane" is a beautiful poem in *Book of Songs*, which praises the graceful and peaceful atmosphere of the prosperous times. Perhaps it is the name that destines it will not be easily damaged.

避暑山庄

　　宫殿区恪守规制，代表着国家的权威与庄重的一面。而被山水围绕的苑景区更像是悠然唯美的画卷，褪去威严，开始寻觅美与意境的存在。

The Palace Area abides by regulations, representing the authority and solemnity of the country. While the Garden Area surrounded by mountains and rivers is more like a leisurely and beautiful picture scroll, whose its majesty fades away and begins to look for the existence of beauty and artistic conception.

　　"山庄胜趣，实在一水。"山庄的湖区总称塞湖，被大小洲屿分隔成形式各异、意趣不同的九个湖面，以长堤、小桥、曲径等纵横相连。湖区建筑多用分散布局手法，园中有园，每组建筑都形成独立的小天地。

"Chengde Mountain Resort wins in the water". The Lake Area of Chengde Mountain Resort, collectively known as Saihu Lake, was divided into nine lakes with different forms and interest and charms by large or small islands, which were connected by long dikes, small bridges and winding paths. The buildings in the Lake Area were mostly scattered in layout, with garden in a garden, and each group of buildings formed an independent small world.

　　这里是皇帝理想中的诗境，大江南北的名胜景观在这里荟萃，亭、榭、楼、阁各色建筑具备，浓缩着中华锦绣大地上的精彩，它是皇帝的梦想园林，也是中国的梦幻名片。那些自北方而来的少数民族首领、那些自海外而来的各国使节，从这里感受到了地大物博的锦绣中华到底有多不可思议。

Here it was the Emperors' ideal poetic landscape, where the scenic spots north and south of the Yangtze River gather together, and where there were a variety of buildings including pavilions, terraces and towers, concentrating the splendor of the beautiful land of China. It was the Emperors' dream garden, and the dream card of China as well. Those minority leaders from the north and those envoys from foreign countries, from here, felt how incredible the splendid China was with the vast territory and abundant resources.

　　避暑山庄最早动工兴建的芝径云堤，仿杭州西湖苏堤的神韵而建。芝径云堤北端是如意洲，这里的建筑以严整朴素的北方民居格调见长。如意洲北端相连一座小岛，岛上仿浙江嘉兴烟雨楼的形制修建了一组楼房，也名为烟雨楼。在湖水的升华中，烟雨楼云蒸霞蔚，蔚为壮观，及至午间则水波映照，晴光荡漾。

Zhijing Yundi (Fairy-herb Path and Cloudy Causeway), was first built in Chengde Mountain Resort, imitating the charm of the Sudi Causeway of the West Lake in Hangzhou. The north end of Zhijing Yundi is Ruyi Island, where the buildings were characterized by neat and simple style of the northern folk houses. The north end of Ruyi Island was connected to a small island, on which a group of buildings were built in the shape of Yanyu Lou in Jiaxing of Zhejiang Province, also named Yanyu Lou (House of Mist and Rain). In the sublimation of the lake water, Yanyu Lou was magnificent with rosy clouds slowing rising, and at noon, the water wave ripples, shimmering in the sunshine.

世界文化遗产

山庄的文津阁和北京紫禁城内的文渊阁、圆明园的文源阁、沈阳故宫的文溯阁合称"内廷四阁"，是清代的四座皇家藏书楼。书最怕起火，藏书阁名称带水，以水克火。

Wenjinge (Knowledge Imparting Hall) in Chengde Mountain Resort, Wenyuange in the Forbidden City in Beijing, Wenyuange in the Summer Palace (the Imperial Garden burnt by British and French troops in 1860) and Wensuge in the Imperial Palace in Shenyang were collectively known as the "Four Halls of the Imperial Palaces", which were the four imperial libraries of the Qing Dynasty. Books were most afraid of fire. There was water elements in the Chinese characters of the name of the libraries, in order to overcome fire.

大塞之北
世界文化遗产

　　文津阁的营造法式仿自浙江宁波大藏书家范钦所建的"天一阁"。此阁处于山环水抱之中，阁楼明为二层，实为三层，中间一层是暗层，为藏书之用。阁内曾储有《四库全书》和《古今图书集成》各一部。

The construction of Wenjinge was modelled on the "Tianyige", the Private Knowledge Imparting Hall built by Fan Qin, a great bibliophile in Ningbo of Zhejiang Province. Surrounded by mountains and lakes, it was a two-storey building, but actually it is three-storey, with the middle as a blind storey for collecting books. There was once stored a collection of the *Siku Quanshu* or *Complete Library in the Four Branches of Literature*, and *Gujin Tushu Jicheng* or *Collection of Ancient and Modern Books*.

　　金山岛仿照镇江金山所建，又有自己的创造。镇江金山寺"山裹寺"，寺院、亭台皆在山坳中，不转弯进山就看不见。而山庄的金山布局是"寺裹山"，金山为建筑所遮掩，一眼看过去只见楼宇不见山。这种仿中有创、独出心裁的设计，在山庄建筑中俯拾皆是。

Jinshan Islet was modelled after Jinshan Hill in Zhenjiang of Jiangsu Province, but had its own creation. In Jinshan Temple in Zhenjiang, "hills surround the temple", where temples and pavilions were in the col, and they could not be seen if visitors did not turn into the hill. While in Jinshan Islet in Chengde Mountain Resort, "temples surround the hills", where the hills were hidden by buildings, and only the buildings could be seen but not hills at a glance. This kind of creative and unique design in imitation could be found everywhere in the buildings of Chengde Mountain Resort.

　　更为难得的是金山脚下，一处处生态趣景跃然湖面。红色的蜻蜓流连戏水，悠闲的小鱼遨游在涟漪之间。而当蜻蜓们双宿双飞、嬉戏点水之际，它们浑然不觉来自水下的危机却在缓缓逼近。动物们弱肉强食的残酷与山水相间的山庄盛景，对于专门跑到山庄来摄影的发烧友们，却是美丽的瞬间。

　　What is rarer is that at the foot of Jinshan Hill, there is an interesting ecological scene on the lake, with red dragonflies playing on the water, and leisurely fish swimming in the ripples. While the dragonflies are flying in pairs and skimming the water, they are not aware that the crisis from underwater is slowly approaching. The cruelty of the law of the jungle among animals and the magnificent scenery of mountains and lakes in Chengde Mountain Resort are beautiful moments for the enthusiasts who come here to take photos.

乾隆帝一生多次南巡，到苏州时，他钟情于那里的狮子园，于是命画师照实画图纪录，在山庄内仿建，这就是文园狮子林。方寸之间，太湖石为山为壑，为丘为岭，崎岖多姿，建筑精巧玲珑，深具元代大画家倪瓒笔下的狮子林图的神韵。

Emperor Qianlong visited the south many times in his life. When he arrived in Suzhou, he loved the Lion Grove Garden there very much. So he commanded a painter to draw and record according to the real scene and copied it in Chengde Mountain Resort. This is Wenyuan Shizilin (the Lion Forest Garden), where Taihu Lake stone was used for the mountains and valleys, for the hills and ridges, rugged and colorful. With exquisite architectures, it has the spirit and charm of the Lion Grove Garden painted by Ni Zan, a great painter in the Yuan Dynasty.

　　"水流云在"是一座大型敞亭，重檐是它的最大特色，第一层飞檐挑出十二个角，顶檐四个角，俗称"十六角亭"。飞檐层层相覆，翘角错落有致，既是蓄势待发的能量，也是缤纷绚丽的幻梦。亭的名称取自杜甫《江亭》诗句"水流心不竞，云在意俱迟"，意思是溪水长流、浮云永在、我心悠然。

　　"Shuiliu Yunzai (Flowing Water and Floating Clouds)" is a large open pavilion, with double eaves as its biggest feature. The first layer of cornices has twelve corners, and the top eaves four corners, which is commonly known as the "Sixteen-Corner Pavilion". With the cornices layer by layer, and the corners well-arranged, it is not only the energy accumulated to start out, but also the colorful dream. The name of the pavilion comes from Du Fu's poem *River Pavilion*: "The water flows on, my heart does not contend; The white clouds drift slowly, as leisurely as my mind", which means that the stream is flowing, the clouds are always there, and I just take things easy.

大东北
世界文化遗产

　　观莲所，依水静坐。相传孩童时期的乾隆，曾在这里流利地背诵出了《爱莲说》，赢得康熙的青睐，为日后能够继承大统增添了情感的砝码。

Guanlian Suo (Pavilion for Watching Lotus), is a place where one can sit quietly by the water. Legend has it that Emperor Qianlong recited *Ode to Lotus Flower* fluently here when he was still a child, which won the favor of Emperor Kangxi and added emotional weight to his future succession.

　　康熙与乾隆这对祖孙，除了都对避暑山庄情有独钟外，还有另一个共同爱好——钟表。如今山庄博物馆的钟表展厅内就存有多架康乾时期的精美钟表。

Emperor Kangxi and Emperor Qianlong, the grandfather and grandson, in addition to their love for Chengde Mountain Resort, had another thing in common: love for clocks. Now there are many exquisite clocks of the Kangxi and Qianlong periods in the Clock Exhibition Hall of Chengde Mountain Resort Museum.

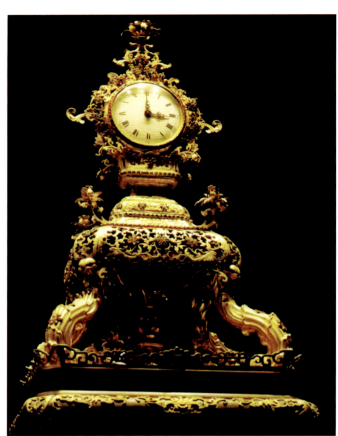

中国是世界上最早发明计时器的国家之一，在古代我国普遍使用"滴漏"和"日晷"作为计时器。明万历年间，"自鸣钟"传入中国。康乾时期，皇帝们更是把钟表视作高雅的珍玩来崇尚。

China is one of the first countries in the world to invent a timer. In ancient China, "hourglass" and "sundial" were widely used as timers. During the reign of Emperor Wanli of the Ming Dynasty, the "chime clock" was introduced into China. During the period of Emperor Kangxi and Qianlong, they regarded clocks as elegant rare curios.

这里展出的钟表有一部分来自于欧洲，造型、装饰都异国情调十足。还有一部分则是由清宫廷造办处修造。

Some of the clocks displayed here came from Europe, with exotic shapes and decorations, and some were made by the Palace Workshops of the Qing Dynasty.

这座铜镀金花架表，就是出产于乾隆时期的广州，铜镀金材质，整体为花架承托花枝形状，通体镂空缠枝莲纹，镶嵌各色料石，造型玲珑秀美。紫檀木束腰底座，上嵌铜镀金装饰，顶装圆形表盘，四周缠绕花卉，尖顶为盛开的莲花，呼应着多水多莲的山庄之景。

This gold-plated copper clock with flower-shaped frame was produced in Guangzhou during Qianlong's reign. It was made of gold-plated copper, with flower-shaped frame supporting flower branches. The whole body was hollowed out with interlaced lotus patterns and inlaid with a variety of processed stones, in an exquisite and beautiful shape. Red sandalwood base was inlaid with gold-plated copper decoration, and the round dial was on the top, surrounded by flowers. The pointed top was a blooming lotus, echoing the scenery of water and lotus in Chengde Mountain Resort.

山庄康乾72景，有31景在湖区。正如莹心堂门殿上的题联所言"自有山川连北极，天然风景胜西湖"，精辟地概括了山庄的精神气质。

In Chengde Mountain Resort there are 72 scenic sites named by Emperor Kangxi and Qianlong, 31 of which are in the Lake Area. As the inscription on the gate of Yingxin Tang (Hall of Clear Heart) says, "there are mountains and rivers connected to the North Pole, and the natural sceneries are better than the West Lake", which incisively summarizes the spiritual temperament of Chengde Mountain Resort.

湖区以北的大片平地便是平原区，这片被热河冲积而成的平原，水源充沛，土地肥沃。万树园更是碧草如茵、草丰木茂。早在避暑山庄建立之前，这里就是蒙古人的牧场。作为重要政治活动的场所，康熙、乾隆、嘉庆曾经多次在这里会见、宴请少数民族王公贵族以及来自东南亚与欧洲的各国使节。

The large flat area on the north of the Lake Area is the Plain Area, which is formed by the alluvium of the Rehe River, with abundant water resources and fertile land. Wanshuyuan (Garden of Ten Thousand Trees), is covered with a carpet of green grass and luxuriant plants and trees. Long before the construction of Chengde Mountain Resort, it was the pasture of the Mongols. As a place for important political activities, Emperor Kangxi, Qianlong and Jiaqing met and entertained the lords and nobles of ethnic minorities as well as envoys from Southeast Asia and Europe here for many times.

1792年9月，乾隆帝在万树园会见英国使臣马戛尔尼。因为礼仪问题，双方曾展开了多次针锋相对的争论。最终，马戛尔尼并未按清廷的要求行叩拜之礼，乾隆帝也勉强接见了他们。不过，乾隆拒绝了英国人提出的中英之间展开贸易谈判的请求，就连他们带来的礼物也被搁置一旁，这些礼物代表了当时英国科技和工业发展的最高水平。此时高高在上的乾隆帝不会想到，他的这一拒绝，或许让中国错失了一次融入世界工业潮流的良机。

In September 1792, Emperor Qianlong met with George Macartney, a British envoy, in Wanshuyuan. There had been many tit-for-tat arguments over etiquette problems. In the end, Macartney did not bow to the Emperor as required by the Qing Dynasty, and Emperor Qianlong reluctantly received them. However, Qianlong refused the British request for trade negotiations between China and Britain, and even the gifts they brought were put aside, which represented the highest level of technological and industrial development in Britain at that time. Emperor Qianlong, who stood high above the masses at that time, would not have thought that his refusal might have missed a good opportunity for China to integrate into the world industrial trend.

万树园正北有一座八角九层楼阁式砖塔，这是永佑寺舍利塔，模仿杭州六和塔而建。舍利塔突破了万树园的横野平空，让山庄整个空间有了层次感。

There is an octagonal nine-storey pavilion-style brick pagoda in the north of Wanshuyuan, which is the Stupa of Yongyou Temple, imitating the Liuhe Pagoda (Pagoda of Six Harmonies) in Hangzhou. The Stupa breaks through the horizontal space of Wanshuyuan, giving the whole Chengde Mountain Resort a sense of spatial level.

避暑山庄近八成的面积是山区。比起其他
园林以土石堆砌的假山装点，避暑山庄以一大
片连绵不断的真实山岭为景致，可谓是大国大
手笔。依山就势，大量建筑与山峰、峡谷、崖
畔、水涧巧妙融合，人与自然结合紧密，天人
合一。

Nearly eighty percent of Chengde Mountain
Resort is mountainous area. Compared with other
gardens, which are decorated with rockeries built
with earth and rocks, Chengde Mountain Resort
takes a vast stretch of real mountains as its scenery, which can be described as a grand work of a
great power. Along the mountains, a large number
of buildings are skillfully integrated with peaks,
canyons, cliffs and streams. Man and nature are
so closely integrated that man becomes an integral
part of nature.

　　磬峰落照是座亭子，聚焦的是山庄东面的磬锤峰。磬锤峰是中国丹霞地貌的标志，形成于300万年前，上粗下细，遗世独立，可与非洲纳米比亚的"上帝拇指"相媲美。虽然它挺立在山庄外的群山中，但在山庄肇建之初就将它规划进来，成为一处景观。这是中国建筑独特的创意手法"借景"。

　　Qingfeng Luozhao (Sunset View of Qingchui Peak) is the name of a pavilion, focusing on the Qingchui Peak or the Hammer Peak in the east of Chengde Mountain Resort. Hammer Peak is the symbol of Danxia landform in China, and was formed three million years ago. It is thick at the top and thin at the bottom. Standing aloof from the world, it is on a par with the "God's Thumb" in Namibia, Africa. Although it stands in the mountains outside Chengde Mountain Resort, it was planned to become a landscape at the very beginning of the construction of Chengde Mountain Resort. This is the unique creative technique of "view borrowing" in Chinese architecture.

四面云山亭最适合观景，它位于西山的最高处，不仅可以俯瞰避暑山庄及周边寺庙的全貌，还将整个承德的丹霞地貌圈尽收眼底，僧冠山、蛤蟆石，诸峰竞秀。每当九九重阳之日，乾隆帝都亲率近臣、各族首领在这里登高野宴。

Simian Yunshan (Pavilion Among Clouds and Mountains) is the most suitable place for sightseeing. Located at the highest point of the Western Hills, it not only overlooks the whole scenery of Chengde Mountain Resort and the surrounding temples, but also has a panoramic view of the Danxia landform circle in Chengde, where Sengguan Mountain, Frog Rock and other peaks competing for beauty. Whenever the day of the Double Ninth Festival on the 9th day of the 9th lunar month came, Emperor Qianlong would personally lead his close ministers and national leaders to climb the mountain and have a picnic here.

从南向北，山区还分布着四道峡谷，松云峡、梨树峪、松林峪、榛子峪，沿着峡谷，各具风韵的景观逶迤排列，与山势林木融为一体，和谐之象浑然天成。

From south to north, there are also four canyons in the mountain area, namely Pine Cloud Gorge, Pear Tree Valley, Pinewood Valley and Hazelnut Valley. Along the canyon, the landscapes with different charms are arranged, which are integrated into the mountains and trees, and the image of harmony is just like nature itself.

山水林间，常有翡翠小鸟光顾，它们的羽毛多为鲜艳的蓝绿色，即使脱落也不会褪色。这一特性成就了我国一项传统手工艺——点翠。

In the mountains, rivers and forests, kingfishers can be often seen. Their feathers are mostly bright blue-green, and even if they fall off, their color will not fade. This feature has contributed to the Kingfisher Craft, a traditional handicraft in China using kingfishers' feathers for ornament.

山庄博物馆珍藏的这件钿翠花鸟挂屏，紫檀边框上浮雕缠枝花卉纹，内侧嵌饰的便是由翠鸟羽毛黏合而成的石榴树、鸟、山石、竹、菊等图案，色彩亮丽、鲜艳。如今，随着翠鸟成为国家二级保护动物，点翠工艺也日渐沉寂，只有留存下来的文物还在诉说着这种工艺的独特与美丽。

The Hanging Screen with Flowers and Birds Designs Inlaid with Mother-of-pearl was collected by Chengde Mountain Resort Museum, the red sandalwood frame was decorated in relief with twining floral patterns, and the inside was decorated with patterns of pomegranate trees, birds, stones, bamboos and chrysanthemums glued together with kingfisher feathers, which were bright and colorful. Nowadays, as the kingfisher has become a national second-class protected animal, the handicraft using kingfisher's feather for ornament is gradually dying, and only the remaining cultural relics are still telling about its uniqueness and beauty.

　　山巅谷底，曾是清帝演练骑射的场所，清代画家就曾为乾隆帝画过一幅《乾隆皇帝一箭双麀图》。今天，野生的梅花鹿或穿梭，或流连，如同三百年前一般矫健。当康乾盛世成为过去，它们不再是围猎中被追猎的对象，山庄也不再是清王朝辉煌岁月的承载者。

The top of the mountain and the bottom of the valley were once the place where the Emperors of the Qing Dynasty practiced riding and shooting. There was a painter in the Qing Dynasty who drew a picture of *Emperor Qianlong Hitting Two Sika Deer with One Arrow*. Today, the wild sika deer either shuttle or linger, as vigorous as it was three hundred years ago. When the prosperous period of Emperor Kangxi and Qianlong passed, they were no longer the target of hunting, and Chengde Mountain Resort was no longer the bearer of the glorious years of the Qing Dynasty.

　　王朝沉沦，建筑无言，这里的每一栋建筑都镌刻着一段历史，每一处风景都有一个意味深远的象征。见过历史的风起云涌，经过岁月的幽深漫长，建筑凝结成语言和思想，穿越时空，带着一个时代无法磨灭的记忆，传递着一如既往的诗情画意。避暑山庄，就这样成为一座由政治、历史、建筑与艺术造就的不朽传奇。

Dynasties sink while buildings are silent. Every building here is engraved with a period of history. Every landscape has a meaningful symbol. Having seen the surging of history and experienced the ups and downs in the long past, the architecture condenses into language and thought, through time and space, conveying the poetic charm as ever, with the indelible memory of an era. Chengde Mountain Resort, in this way, has become an immortal legend created by politics, history, architecture and art.

避暑山庄

3

North of the Great River: World Cultural Heritage

The Eight Outer Temples

外八庙

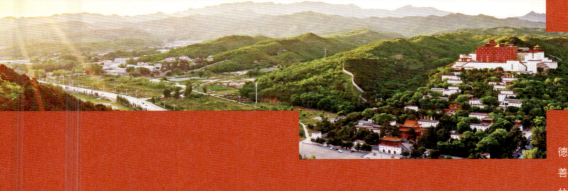

康乾年间，清廷先后在承德避暑山庄周围修造溥仁寺、溥善寺、普宁寺等十二座规模宏伟的皇家寺庙。这些庙宇融汇中国汉、藏、蒙等多民族建筑艺术的精华，在这里，和谐包容、兼容并蓄的胸怀以建筑的形式呈现。在这其中，有八座庙宇由朝廷派驻喇嘛，因位于京师之外，俗称"外八庙"。外八庙在避暑山庄四周以众星拱月之势构筑起了中国最为宏伟集中的寺庙群。"合内外之心，成巩固之业。"避暑山庄及其周围寺庙创造性地解决了中国历史上民族分裂的难解之结，促进了中华民族的大融合。

自东汉年间佛教传入中国以来，庙宇便开始丰富着中国传统文化与建筑艺术。

Since the introduction of Buddhism to China in the Eastern Han Dynasty, temples have enriched Chinese traditional culture and architectural art.

康乾年间，清廷先后在承德避暑山庄周围修造溥仁寺、溥善寺、普宁寺等十二座规模宏伟的皇家寺庙。这些庙宇融汇中国汉、藏、蒙等多民族建筑艺术的精华，在这里，和谐包容、兼容并蓄的胸怀以建筑的形式呈现。在这其中，有八座庙宇由朝廷派驻喇嘛，因位于京师之外，俗称"外八庙"。

During the reign of Emperors Kangxi and Qianlong in the Qing Dynasty, the Government of the Qing Dynasty successively built twelve magnificent imperial temples around Chengde Mountain Resort, including Puren Temple, Pushan Temple and Puning Temple. These temples integrate the essence of Han nationality, Tibetan, Mongolian and other multi-ethnic architectural arts, where the harmonious, inclusive and all-embracing mind was presented in the form of architecture. There were Lamas accredited by the imperial government in eight of the temples, which were commonly known as the "Eight Outer Temples" because they are located outside the capital.

外八庙在避暑山庄四周以众星拱月之势构筑起了中国最为宏伟集中的寺庙群。"合内外之心，成巩固之业。"避暑山庄及其周围寺庙创造性地解决了中国历史上民族分裂的难解之结，促进了中华民族的大融合。

Around Chengde Mountain Resort, the Eight Outer Temples form the most magnificent and concentrated temple cluster in China, like a myriad of stars surrounding the moon. As a Chinese saying goes, "Unite the inside and the outside and achieve the great cause of consolidation." The Chengde Mountain Resort and its surrounding temples creatively solved the difficult problem of ethnic division in Chinese history and promoted the great integration of the Chinese nation.

　　当四方来朝，在新建的庙宇中虔诚礼佛时，当藏传佛教的经文声回荡在山岚雾霭中，避暑山庄与外八庙一起开创了民族团结与文化交融的典范。这里上演了一幕幕促进各民族守望相助、和睦共生的感人故事，随着史册，流传至今。

When people from all directions came to worship Buddha piously in the newly-built temples, when the chanting of Tibetan Buddhist sutras echoed in the mist of the mountains, the Chengde Mountain Resort and the Eight Outer Temples created a model of national unity and cultural integration. A series of touching stories have been staged here to promote the mutual help and harmonious coexistence of all ethnic groups, which have been handed down to this day with the annals of history.

公元1713年，避暑山庄修建后的第十年。这一年，清王朝迎来一件大事，康熙帝的六十寿辰。此时的国家进入又一个发展时期，承德也因为避暑山庄的兴建而日渐繁盛。

In 1713, the tenth year after the construction of the Chengde Mountain Resort, the Qing Dynasty was to welcome an important event, the 60th birthday of Emperor Kangxi. At this time, the country entered another period of development. Chengde became increasingly prosperous with the construction of Chengde Mountain Resort.

蒙古各部落首领从漠北前来朝贺，并恳请出资建庙以铭记恩典，康熙帝应允了这个请求。

Mongol tribal leaders came from North of the Gobi desert to congratulate him and asked for moncy to build a temple in memory of his grace. Emperor Kangxi granted the request.

大不连北
世界文化遗产

很快，溥仁寺便出现在了武烈河的东岸，这是康熙帝在承德修建的第一座寺庙。与后来所建寺庙不同，溥仁寺是典型的汉式庙宇，伽蓝七殿的规整格局，沿着中轴线，山门、天王殿、慈云普荫殿、宝相长新殿依次排列。天王殿上挂着康熙帝亲题的寺名"溥仁"，用蒙、汉、满三种文字书写，意为天下百姓都能享受到皇帝的仁德。

　　Soon, Puren Temple appeared on the east bank of Wulie River, which was the first temple built by Emperor Kangxi in Chengde. Different from the temples built later, Puren Temple was built in typical Han style, with the regular pattern of the seven halls of a temple, along the central axis, the Gate of the Temple, the Hall of Heavenly Kings, Ciyun Puyin Hall and Baoxiang Changxin Hall were arranged successively. Hanging on the Hall of Heavenly Kings was the name of the temple "Puren" inscribed by Emperor Kangxi, which was written in the three languages of Mongolian, Chinese and Manchu, meaning that all people in the world can enjoy the benevolence of the Emperor.

大承德
世界文化遗产

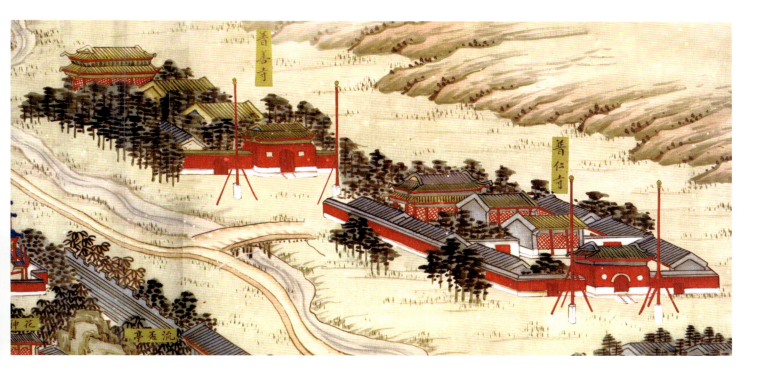

　　据记载，虔诚贺寿的蒙古王公们筹措了20万两白银来修建溥仁寺，但最终只用了10万两，余下来的银两修造了溥善寺。溥善寺位于溥仁寺之后，形制与溥仁寺大体相同，历经动荡，今已不存。

　　It is recorded that the Mongol lords who were devout celebrants of longevity raised 200,000 taels of silver to build Puren Temple, but only 100,000 taels were used in the end, and the remaining money was used to build Pushan Temple. Pushan Temple was behind Puren Temple, with the shape and structure roughly the same as that of Puren Temple, but it disappeared after turmoils.

　　溥仁寺拉开了清廷在承德大规模兴建寺庙的帷幕，庙宇的营建在此后长达七十多年的岁月里从未停止。寒来暑往，庙宇的数目在不断增加，从汉式到藏式，格局愈加宏大。供奉的佛像变换着容颜，色彩日益艳丽，建筑愈发精妙，融合了各民族不同的建筑风格与特点，创造出诸多此前并未出现过的建筑手法，寺庙群落变得前所未有的恢弘与盛大。

　　Puren Temple opened the curtain of the large-scale construction of temples in Chengde by the Government of the Qing Dynasty, which continued for more than 70 years. With the passage of time, the number of temples increased. From Han style to Tibetan style, the temples became grander. The facial appearance of the Buddhist statues enshrined and worshipped in the temples also changed, and became increasingly colorful. The buildings became more and more exquisite, integrating different architectural styles and characteristics of different nationalities, creating many architectural techniques that had never appeared before.The temple complex became unprecedentedly grand and magnificent.

公元1755年，清廷平定准噶尔，厄鲁特蒙古部来归。当年十月，乾隆帝在避暑山庄大宴厄鲁特蒙古部诸位首领。为纪念这次会面，乾隆帝决定仿照康熙帝与喀尔喀蒙古会盟建立多伦汇宗寺的先例，在避暑山庄东北兴建普宁寺。这是乾隆帝继位后在承德修建的第一座佛寺。

In 1755, the Qing Dynasty pacified Dzungaria and the Oirat Mongol tribe submitted to the authority of Qing Dynasty. In October that year, Emperor Qianlong held a grand banquet at Chengde Mountain Resort for the leaders of the Olot Mongol Tribe. In order to commemorate this meeting, Emperor Qianlong decided to build Puning Temple on the northeast of Chengde Mountain Resort, following the precedent of the establishment of Huizong Temple in Duolun by Emperor Kangxi when he made an alliance with Khalkha Mongols. This was the first Buddhist temple built in Chengde after Emperor Qianlong succeeded to the throne.

在乾隆帝亲自撰写的普宁寺碑记中透露出仿造的意义："蒙古向敬佛，兴黄教，故寺之式，即依西藏三摩耶庙之式为之。"黄教，即藏传佛教格鲁派。三摩耶庙，今译为桑耶寺，是西藏第一座具备佛、法、僧三宝的正规寺院，在藏传佛教界拥有崇高的地位。

In the inscription of Puning Temple written by Emperor Qianlong himself, the significance of the imitation was revealed: "Mongolia worships Buddha and promotes the Yellow Sect, so the style of the temple is modeled after Samaya Temple in Tibet." The Yellow Sect was the Gelugpa school of Tibetan Buddhism. Samaya Temple, now translated as Samye Monastery, was the first regular monastery in Tibet with the Triratna of Buddha, Dharma and Sangha, and held a high position in Tibetan Buddhist circles.

一年后，兼具汉藏两种建筑风格的普宁寺落成。"安其居，乐其业，永永普宁。"这一次匾额上面增加了藏文，由满、汉、蒙、藏四种文字题写。

A year later, Puning Temple, which combined both Han and Tibetan architectural styles, was completed. "Living and working in peace and contentment, and the world will be always peaceful." This time, Tibetan characters were added on the horizontal board, which was inscribed in the four languages of Manchu, Han, Mongolian and Tibetan.

普宁寺前半部分是汉式形制，大雄宝殿坐落在高台之上，高台是权力、正统、荣耀的标志。大殿前的台阶镶嵌双龙戏珠丹陛石，象征至高无上。

The first half of Puning Temple was built in Han style. The Main Hall, or the Mahavira Hall, was located on the high platform, which was the symbol of power, legitimism and glory. In the middle of the steps in front of the hall there was a big rectangular stone inlaid with two dragons frolicking with a pearl, symbolizing supremacy.

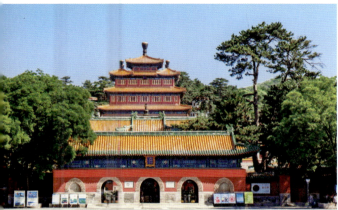

越过大雄宝殿，高台之上白塔红墙，别有洞天。在佛教经典中，世界中心有座须弥山。因此，在佛国，佛、菩萨的造像都供奉在须弥台座之上。普宁寺的主体建筑大乘之阁象征着须弥山，仿照桑耶寺乌策殿而建，两侧配有日月两殿，象征太阳、月亮围绕须弥山出没。大殿四角分别修建四座喇嘛塔，代表密宗的"四智"。东西南北四方矗立着四座台殿，象征四大部洲，四大部洲周边有八座重层白台，象征八小部洲，代表宇宙四面八方。这种统一向心的布局是典型的藏式佛教建筑坛城，也叫曼陀罗。普宁寺的曼陀罗是我国寺庙中目前保存最为完整的一个。

Across the Mahavira Hall, the white pagoda and red walls on the high platform made an altogether different world. In the Buddhist scriptures, there was Mount Sumeru in the center of the world. Therefore, in the land purified by Buddhism, the statues of Buddha and Bodhisattva are enshrined on the Sumeru pedestal. The Mahayana Pavillion, the main building of Puning Temple, symbolized Mount Sumeru. It was built in the style of the Uce Hall of Samye Monastery, with two Halls of the Sun and the Moon on both sides, symbolizing that the sun and the moon would rise and set around Mount Sumeru. Four Lamaist Pagodas were built at the four corners of the Hall, representing the "four wisdoms" of Tantrism. In the four directions of the east, west, south and north, there were four halls on terraces, symbolizing Caturdvipa, the Four Continents. Around the Four Continents, there were eight double-layer white terraces, symbolizing the Eight Small Continents, and representing the universe in all directions. This centripetal layout was a typical Tibetan Buddhist architecture known as Mandala. The Mandala of Puning Temple was the best preserved one in China.

　　大乘之阁中心为空井，那是特为千手千眼观世音菩萨立身留出的空间。佛像由松、柏、杉、榆、椴五种木材合雕而成，高22米，体态优美，衣袂飘飘。大佛共有四十二只手臂，除胸前合十的双手外，其余四十只手都持有法器且手心各有一只眼睛。这是世界上最大最重的一尊木雕佛像。

The center of the Mahayana Pavilion was an empty well, which was specially reserved for the standing figure of the Avalokitesvara Bodhisattva with a thousand hands and a thousand eyes. The figure was carved from five kinds of wood, namely pine, cypress, fir, elm and Chinese linden. It was 22 meters high, with graceful posture and fluttering clothes, and a total of forty-two arms. Except for the two hands folded in the front, the other forty hands all held magic instruments used in a Buddhist and each had an eye in the palm. This was the largest and heaviest wooden Buddha figure in the world.

每年立冬前后，正午的某一刻，大殿透入的太阳光线会与观音额前的慧眼相重合。

Every year around the Beginning of Winter, at a certain moment of noon, the rays of sunlight coming through the hall coincide with the Buddha's eyes which perceive both past and future in front of the forehead.

一低头，刹那千年。再回首，沧海桑田。

At a bow of the head, a thousand years passed; looked back, things have greatly changed.

今天的普宁寺是中国北方最大的佛事活动场所。每一天，庙宇在钟声与诵经声中苏醒。钟磬和鸣，梵呗声声。

Today, Puning Temple is the largest Buddhist activity site in northern China. Every day, the temple awakens to the sound of bells and chanting. The bells chime harmoniously and Buddhist chanting of prayers is heard all over.

普宁寺的东边是普佑寺。普佑寺修建之前，承德已有三座皇家寺庙。清政府在普宁寺旁建立了供喇嘛学习研究、精进佛法的札仓，即后来的普佑寺。普佑寺是清朝鼎盛时期全国仅有的两所喇嘛经学院之一，另一所是北京的雍和宫。

Puyou Temple is to the east of Puning Temple. Before the construction of Puyou Temple, there were three royal temples in Chengde. Next to Puning Temple, the Government of the Qing Dynasty established Dratsang for Lamas to study and develop Buddhism, later known as Puyou Temple, which was one of only two Lamaism Institutes in the whole country during the heyday of the Qing Dynasty, the other was Yonghe Lamasery in Beijing.

1964年，因雷击起火，普佑寺的大部分建筑毁于火灾。现存的东西配殿展出着176尊造型各异的罗汉像。这些罗汉像原本有508尊，供奉在承德的另一座寺庙罗汉堂。罗汉堂命运多舛，先被日军占据，后被拆毁。几经波折，罗汉像被转移至普佑寺。这组雕像是我国木雕罗汉的上乘之作。其中不乏介子推、济公等民间家喻户晓的人物。

In 1964, most of the buildings of Puyou Temple were destroyed by a fire due to lightning stroke. In the existing East and West Side Halls, there exhibit 176 sculptures of Arhats in different shapes. The sculptures, originally 508 in number, were enshrined in an Arhat Hall of another temple in Chengde, which was ill-fated. It was first occupied by the Japanese invaders and then demolished. After several twists and turns, the Arhats were transferred to Puyou Temple. This set of carving was the best wood-carving Arhats in China, among which, there were many well-known folk figures such as Jie Zitui and Jigong the Mad Monk, etc.

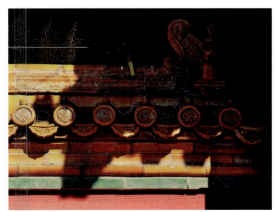

清朝初年，在新疆伊犁河的北岸坐落着一座固尔扎庙，这是清代西北地区蒙古族规模最大的一座寺庙。阿穆尔撒纳叛乱时，固尔扎庙被焚毁。清军平叛后，1759年，厄鲁特蒙古达什达瓦部两千多人从伊犁迁居热河。1764年，乾隆下令依照新疆的固尔扎庙修建安远庙，作为达什达瓦部从事宗教活动的场所。安远庙集蒙古族建筑与汉式建筑风格于一体。

In the early years of the Qing Dynasty, there stood a Gurza Temple on the north bank of the Ili River in Xinjiang. It was the largest Mongolian temple in Northwest China in the Qing Dynasty and was burnt down during the Rebellion of Amur Sana. After the Qing army suppressed the rebellion, more than 2,000 people of Dash Dawa Tribe of the Oirat Mongolia moved from Ili to Rehe in 1759. In 1764, Emperor Qianlong ordered the construction of Anyuan Temple in accordance with the Gurza Temple in Xinjiang as a place for religious activities of the Dash Dawa Tribe. Anyuan Temple was a combination of Mongolian and Han architectural styles.

安远庙，也叫伊犁庙，因主殿普度殿为方形，当地人又称它为方亭子。普度殿建有三重屋檐，屋顶以黑色琉璃瓦覆顶，这在古代寺庙建筑和皇家建筑中极为罕见。古人将宇宙中的天地万物分为五大类，金、木、水、火、土。黑色象征着水，固尔扎庙毁于火，普度殿黑瓦覆顶，意在以水克火。

Anyuan Temple, also known as Ili Temple, was called Square Pavilion by the local people as the main hall, Pudu Hall, was square. Pudu Hall was built with triple eaves and roofed with black glazed tiles, which was extremely rare in ancient temple architecture and imperial buildings. The ancients divided everything in the universe into five categories: metal, wood, water, fire and earth. Black symbolizes water. Gurza Temple was destroyed by fire and so Pudu Hall was roofed with black tiles, which was intended to overcome fire with water.

普度殿是一座艺术的殿堂。殿内供奉的木雕髹漆绿度母像是安远庙的镇寺之宝，佛像高大庄严、体态婀娜，其身后的木雕背光雕镂内容繁多，层次分明。殿顶方形藻井精致繁复，美观华丽。大殿四周的墙壁绘有以绿度母为主题的壁画，现存27幅。人物、建筑、园林、溪涧、山林，色彩秾丽，内容丰富，简洁生动，展示了当时的生产生活场景。

Pudu Hall was a hall of art. The wood carving lacquered Green Tara enshrined in the Hall was the treasure of Anyuan Temple. The statue was tall and solemn, with a graceful posture. The backlight wood carvings behind was rich in contents and distinct in layers. The square caisson ceiling was exquisite and complicated, beautiful and gorgeous. The walls around the main hall were painted with murals with the theme of Green Tara, 27 of which are still in existence. Figures, buildings, gardens, streams, mountains and forests were rich in color as well as content, concise and vivid, showing the production and life scenes at that time.

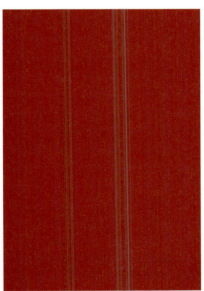

方亭子南边有一座圆亭子，这是修建晚于安远庙两年的普乐寺，其主体建筑旭光阁仿北京天坛祈年殿而建，状为圆形，因而得名。

　　There is a Round Pavilion on the south of the Square Pavilion. It is Pule Temple which was built two years later than Anyuan Temple. Xuguang Pavilion facing the Rising Sun is the main building, which was built in imitation of the Hall of Prayer for Good Harvest of the Temple of Heaven in Beijing and got the name because of its shape.

　　1757年，清王朝彻底平定了准噶尔部。两年后，清军又粉碎了回部霍集占兄弟的暴乱，西北疆更趋稳定，西北各民族与清朝政府的关系也日益密切。1766年，清廷建普乐寺，以便西北各民族首领在承德觐见时礼佛、瞻礼、下榻。"普乐"寓意"天下同乐"。

　　In 1757, the Qing Dynasty completely pacified the Dzungaria tribe, and two years later, the army of Qing Dynasty crushed the riots of the Hojijan brothers of the Hui tribe. The northwest Xinjiang became more stable. The relationship between the northwest nationalities and the Government of the Qing Dynasty became closer and closer. In 1766, the Government of the Qing Dynasty built Pule Temple so that the leaders of all ethnic groups in northwest China could worship Buddha and stay in Chengde when they met the Emperor. "Pule" means "universal happiness".

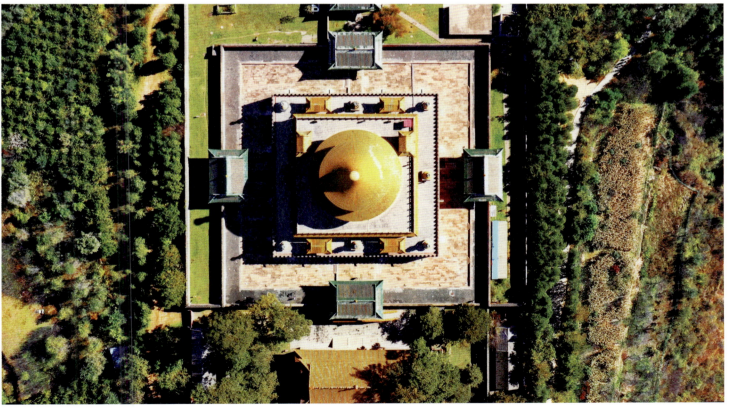

普乐寺的平面、立面都十字对称，是外八庙中布局最严谨的一座。开有两个山门，前山门正对避暑山庄，后山门正对磬锤峰。乾隆帝视磬锤峰为神物，认为它是上天的启示，故在寺后又辟一座山门。这种布局在中国寺庙中比较少见。

　　The plane and elevation of Pule Temple were cross-symmetrical, which was the most rigorous layout of the Eight Outer Temples. There were two gates, the front facing Chengde Mountain Resort and the back facing the Hammer Peak. Emperor Qianlong considered the Hammer Peak sacred, believing that it was a revelation from Heaven, so he built another gate at the back of the temple. This kind of layout was relatively rare in Chinese temples.

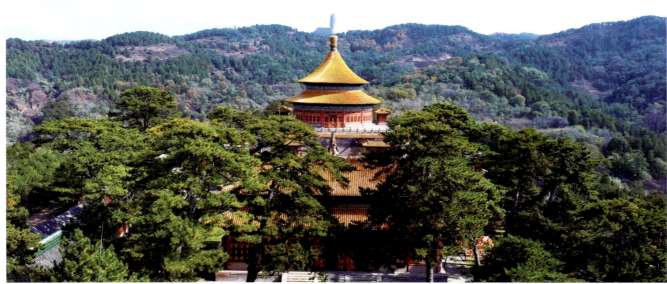

穿过前部规整的七殿，普乐寺后部是一座藏式阁城，最高处是主体建筑旭光阁。方形的阁城，圆形的殿阁，旭光阁体现了天圆地方的中国古代宇宙观。

　　Through the seven regular halls in the front, the rear part of Pule Temple is a Tibetan-style platform, and Xuguang Pavilion, the main building, is at the highest point. With the square platform and circular halls, Xuguang Pavilion embodies the ancient Chinese cosmology of round heaven and square earth.

旭光阁内顶部置有圆形藻井。藻井象征天宇的崇高，在建筑的穹顶之上，升腾着另一种恢宏与神秘。藻井也是中国封建等级制度的标志，一般只用于宫殿和寺庙之中，越尊贵的建筑，藻井越精致繁复。旭光阁的藻井为龙凤藻井，三层重翘重昂九踩斗拱的手法堆砌出极致的艺术之美。

At the top of Xuguang Pavilion, there is a round caisson ceiling, which symbolizes the loftiness of the heaven, and another kind of magnificence and mystery rises above the dome of the building. The caisson ceiling, also a symbol of the feudal hierarchy in China, was only used in palaces and temples generally. The more noble the building, the more elaborate and complicated the caisson ceiling. With patterns of dragon and phoen x, the caisson ceiling of Xuguang Pavilion, adopted the technique of three-layer bucket arch with double petal and double lever and nine extension of bracket, creating the ultimate artistic beauty.

大话冯北
世界文化遗产

1767年，乾隆帝下旨修建普陀宗乘之庙，借此庆祝三年后他的六十寿辰。此时的清王朝进入了鼎盛时期，强盛的国力让乾隆帝有资本实现政治上的远大抱负，他准备用规格远超山庄的寺庙团结藏、蒙等少数民族领袖。以庆寿之名，行怀柔之实。

　　In 1767, Emperor Qianlong ordered the construction of Putuo Zongcheng Temple (Temple of Potarak Doctrine) to celebrate his 60th birthday three years later. At this time, the Qing Dynasty was in its heyday, and the solid national strength gave Emperor Qianlong the capital to fulfill his political ambition. He was ready to unite Tibetan, Mongolian and other ethnic leaders with temples far beyond the standards of Chengde Mountain Resort, trying to bring them under control through conciliation in the name of celebrating his birthday.

普陀宗乘之庙比照西藏的布达拉宫缩小尺寸而建，普陀宗乘就是藏语布达拉的翻译，因此它又称小布达拉宫。如同原版一样，是一个极为庞大的建筑群。模仿中有取舍，比照中有创新。普陀宗乘之庙的六十余处建筑依山就势自由散置，疏密有致。

　　Putuo Zongcheng Temple was built in a size smaller than the Potala Palace in Tibet. Putuo Zongcheng was the translation of Potala in Tibetan, so it was also called the Little Potala Palace. Like the original Potala, it was an enormous building complex. There were trade-offs in imitation and innovations in comparison. More than sixty buildings in Putuo Zongcheng Temple were well spaced, scattering freely along the mountains.

普陀宗乘之庙大手笔投入，耗资近二百万两白银。落成时恰逢土尔扈特部回归，它也顺势成为土尔扈特部回归的纪念碑。不同于避暑山庄青砖灰瓦的低调，普陀宗乘之庙的建筑多用明黄、暗绿的琉璃瓦覆顶，富丽庄重。

　　Putuo Zongcheng Temple was invested with big money, and it spent nearly two million taels of silver. The completion of the Temple coincided with the return of the Turghut tribe, thus it also became a monument to the return of the Turghut tribe. Different from the low-key black bricks and grey tiles of Chengde Mountain Resort, the buildings of Putuo Zongcheng Temple were mostly roofed with bright yellow and dark green glazed tiles, solemn and magnificent.

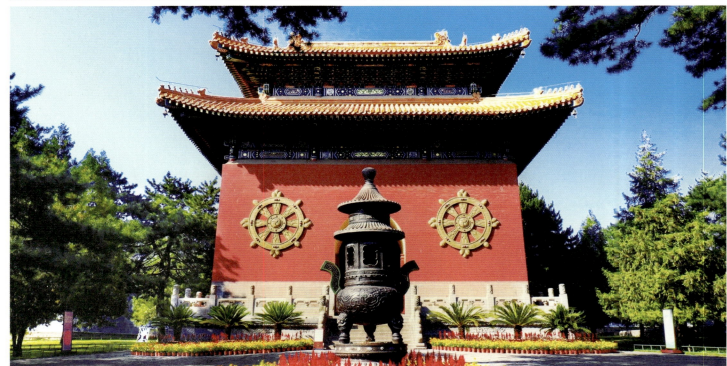

　　藏式白台式山门内，正中为碑亭。碑亭之北是五塔门，顶上有五座造型各异的喇嘛塔，分别代表藏传佛教的五派。

　　The Gate of the Temple is a building with Tibetan White Platform, and the Tablet Pavilion is behind the Gate. To the north of the Pavilion there is the Gate of Five Pagodas, on the top of which are five Lama Pagodas of different shapes, representing the five schools of Tibetan Buddhism.

五塔门后是一座三间四柱七楼形制的汉式琉璃牌坊。顶上七楼，飞檐翘角。檐上端坐着各种神兽，它们是防雷的希望，防火的寄托，承载着风调雨顺、国泰民安的愿望。门额间镶嵌的黄琉璃双龙戏珠图案，昭示着这座牌坊不一般的地位。

　　Behind the Gate of the Five Pagodas there is the Glazed Memorial Archway in Han style with three doors, four columns and seven gable and hip roofs on the top. On the seven roofs, there are upturned eaves, on which various kinds of mythical creatures are seated. They are the hope of lightning protection and fire prevention, bearing the wishes of good weather, prosperity and peace of the country. The pattern of yellow glazed double dragons playing with a pearl inlaid on the top part of the lintel shows the unusual status of this memorial archway.

　　高台，可以观天、望气，并能抬高木建筑，免受水浸。普陀宗乘之庙的主体建筑就在高台之上。大红台通高43米，下部基座大白台用花岗岩砌筑。大红台列窗七层，最下层的汉式横长方形窗与上部藏式梯形窗搭配和谐。正中开有六个琉璃佛龛，内置琉璃佛像。

　　High platform, on which people can watch the sky and observe the clouds (to read the future), raises the wooden building to avoid flooding. The main building of Putuo Zongcheng Temple is on the high platform. The Grand Red Platform is 43 meters high, and the Grand White Platform as the lower base was built with granite. There are seven layers of windows in the Grand Red Platform, and the horizontal rectangular window of the Han style in the lowest layer is in harmony with the Tibetan trapezoidal window in the upper part. There are six niches of colored glaze in the middle, with colored glaze Buddha statues inside.

大红台内部建筑呈"回"字形，主殿就是"回"字中间核心的"口"。

The interior buildings of the Grand Red Platform is in the shape of "回", the homocentric squares The main hall is the central square, the "口" which means "mouth" in Chinese in the center of "回".

在中国古代的观念中，屋顶从来就不是一个简单的建筑元素，体现着等级。主殿重檐四角攒尖顶，繁复而隆重，鲜艳却庄重，是地位的象征。瓦在屋顶之上占据了制高点，瓦的颜色就成为最醒目的建筑礼制标志。主殿殿顶全用鎏金鱼鳞状铜瓦覆盖，排排铺设，如阵势磅礴的兵阵，主殿的庄严与尊贵再一次被着重强调。

In the ancient Chinese concept, the roof has never been a simple architectural element, it reflected the hierarchy. The main hall had double eaves and pyramid roofs, complicated and grand, bright but solemn, which were symbols of status. The tiles occupied the commanding height above the roof, whose color became the most striking symbol of architectural etiquette. The roof of the main hall was covered with gilded fish-scale copper tiles, which were laid in rows, like a might array of troops. The solemnity and dignity of the main hall were emphasized once again.

大承之北
世界文化遗产

主殿名为万法归一。万里东归的土尔扈特部首领渥巴锡，就曾被乾隆帝安排在这里聆听佛法。

The name of the main hall is Wanfa Guiyi, meaning all Buddha Dharmas are one. Ubashi, the leader of the Turghut tribe who had returned thousands of miles to the east, was arranged by Emperor Qianlong to listen to Buddha dharma here.

1933年，普陀宗乘之庙以"承德金庙"的称号为世界所知。此前，瑞典探险家斯文赫定被万法归一殿的宏伟与华丽所震惊。在建筑学家梁思成的帮助下，斯文赫定以1∶1的比例复原了万法归一殿，并将它搭建在芝加哥世博会上。"承德金庙"与"米老鼠和唐老鸭"一起，成为那届世博会最受欢迎的两件展品。

In 1933, Putuo Zongcheng Temple was known to the world with the title of "Chengde Golden Temple". Sven Hedin, a Swedish explorer, was shocked by the grandeur and magnificence of the Hall. With the help of Liang Sicheng, a famous architect in China, Sven Hedin restored the Hall in a 1:1 ratio and built it in Chicago World Expo. Chengde Golden Temple, together with Mickey Mouse and Donald Duck, became the two most popular exhibits at that Expo.

　　斯文赫定阐述过他的复制意图：并不局限于保存建筑自身的价值，而是希望借此纪念十八世纪的土尔扈特部族以及他们史诗般的苦难迁徙，那场跨越亚洲的回归之旅。

　　Sven Hedin had stated his intention to reproduce the Hall: not only to preserve the value of the building itself, but to commemorate the Turghut tribe and their miserable epic migration in the eighteenth century, their journey of return back to China across Asia.

普陀宗乘之庙建成后的数年里，清王朝征讨四方的历史已经过去。乾隆帝终于可以暂时放下怀柔之举，缔造一个自己理想中的帝国。早在前些年，乾隆帝刻意将接待来朝贵宾的场所放在承德，承德已是清王朝与世界沟通的窗口。此前修建的庙宇，多为少数民族藩属所考虑。这一次，乾隆帝开始了自己的创作。

In the years after the completion of Putuo Zongcheng Temple, the history of the Qing Dynasty's conquest of different places had ended. Emperor Qianlong was finally able to temporarily put aside his conciliatory actions and create an ideal empire of his own. As early as a few years before, Emperor Qianlong deliberately arranged the place to receive distinguished guests in Chengde, which was already the window for the Qing Dynasty to communicate with the world. Most of the temples were built for the consideration of the vassal states of ethnic minorities before. This time, Emperor Qianlong began his own creation.

1774年，乾隆帝先后兴建了两座寺院，一座海宁寺，仿浙江海宁寺，今天已无迹可寻。一座殊像寺，仿山西五台山殊像寺而建。

In 1774, Emperor Qianlong built two temples successively. One was Haining Temple, imitating Haining Temple in Zhejiang Province. Today, no trace of it can be found. The other was Shuxiang Temple, modeled on Shuxiang Temple in Wutai Mountain of Shanxi Province.

殊像寺有"乾隆家庙"之称。建在山腰、居高临下的会乘殿是主殿，也是乾隆帝礼佛和藏经的地方。会乘殿之后是以宝相阁为中心的藏式曼陀罗。随着地势陡然升高，大规模堆叠假山，如朵朵祥云。祥云之上，石质须弥座托承着宝相阁。中国的园林艺术与寺庙建筑在这里完美融合。

Shuxiang Temple was known as the "Qianlong Family Temple". Built on the mountainside, Huicheng Hall, which was in the commanding position, was the main hall and also the place where Emperor Qianlong worshipped Buddha and deposited Buddhist scriptures. Behind Huicheng Hall there was a Tibetan mandala centered on Baoxiang Pavilion. As the terrain rises steeply, rockeries are piled up on a large scale, like auspicious clouds. Above the auspicious clouds, the stone base supports Baoxiang Pavilion. Chinese garden art and temple architecture were perfectly integrated here.

岁月与战火残损了这座寺庙，曾经的香火与钟声已经远去，如今的殊像寺在紧闭的山门之后静默无言。

The temple was damaged by time and war. The incense and bells are gone. Today, Shuxiang Temple stands silently behind the closed gate.

殊像寺建成后的第五年，1780年，是乾隆帝七十岁寿辰。远在后藏的六世班禅额尔德尼要来觐见。

The year of 1780, the fifth year after the completion of Shuxiang Temple, was the 70th birthday of Emperor Qianlong. The 6th Panchen Erdeni, who was far away in Tsang, would come to see Emperor Qianlong.

因身处边疆，六世班禅格外重视与中央政府的联系，坚持西藏与中央政府的归属关系。1774年，英国派人会见六世班禅，提出与西藏建立联系、相互通商等请求。六世班禅严词拒绝，申明西藏属于中国领土，一切要听命于中央政府，维护了国家统一的尊严。

Living in the border area, the 6th Panchen Lama attached great importance to his ties with the central government and insisted on the affiliation of Tibet with the central government. In 1774, Britain sent people to meet with the 6th Panchen Lama and asked to establish a connection and trade with Tibet. The 6th Panchen Lama refused him sternly, affirming that Tibet belonged to China and that everything was subject to the orders of the central government. He safeguarded the dignity of national unity.

听到六世班禅前来的消息，乾隆帝极为欣喜，着手为六世班禅修建行宫，模仿班禅在日喀则的扎什伦布寺的形制建造。行宫名为须弥福寿之庙，意思是多福多寿，如意吉祥。这个重任，乾隆帝安排给了自己的亲信军机大臣和珅。和珅精通满、蒙、汉、藏四种语言，精明强干，仅用一年时间就建好了这座占地3万多平方米的行宫。

Hearing that the 6th Panchen Lama would come, Emperor Qianlong was overjoyed and began to build a palace for him, imitating the shape of the Panchen Lama's Tashilhunpo Monastery in Xigaze. The palace was named Xumi Fushou Temple, which meant more happiness and longevity, good luck and auspiciousness. Emperor Qianlong assigned this important task to his trusted follower He Shen, the Grand Minister of State, who was smart and capable and proficient in four languages, namely, Manchu, Mongolian, Han and Tibetan. It took him only one year to build this palace covering an area of more than 30,000 square meters.

乾隆帝的重视在须弥福寿之庙中无处不在。碑亭中的御碑由一只巨大的赑屃背负，昭示此庙的与众不同。大红台是须弥福寿之庙的主体，壁面上辟有三层中国式垂花窗户，窗头上浮嵌琉璃制垂花门头，为大红台的庄严带来一抹灵秀。大红台四角各建有一座小殿，琉璃瓦顶，脊上有吻兽，南面两殿用孔雀，北面两殿用鹿，象征着前程似锦。

Emperor Qianlong's attention and care could be found everywhere in Xumi Fushou Temple. The imperial tablet in the Tablet Pavilion was carried by Bixi, a legendary giant turtle-shaped animal usually taken for the base of huge stone tablet in former times in China, showing that the temple was different from others. The Grand Red Platform was the main building of Xumi Fushou Temple. There were three layers of Chinese-style windows decorated with swags on the wall, and the swag pattern of colored glaze were inlaid at the top of the window, which brought a touch of elegance to the solemnity of the Grand Red Platform. In each of the four corners of the Grand Red Platform there was a small hall, with a roof of colored glazed tiles and animal sculptures at the ends of the roof ridge. Peacocks were on the two halls in the south and deer in the north, symbolizing a bright future.

大红台中央是一座重檐大殿，名为妙高庄严殿，四条屋脊大有乾坤。角脊下端呈龙头状，脊身波状，匍匐金龙两条，大有凌空欲飞之势。八条金龙，姿态各异，静止的造型蕴含巨大的动感。

　　In the center of the Grand Red Platform there is a double-eave hall, which is called Miaogao Zhuangyan Hall (The Hall of Highness and Solemness). There is a lot to be said about its four ridges. The lower end of the ridges at four corners is in the shape of a dragon head, and the ridge is wave-shaped with two creeping golden dragons as if flying high up in the air. The eight golden dragons are of different postures, still but dynamic.

妙高庄严殿方七间，高三层，是六世班禅的讲经之所。乾隆带领六世班禅参观完整座庙宇之后，在这里请六世班禅为自己讲经。讲经之后，六世班禅将自己从西藏日喀则至承德途中每一站对乾隆的祈祷、祝福记录敬献给了乾隆。

Miaogao Zhuangyan Hall, with seven rooms wide and three storeys high, was the place for the 6th Panchen Lama to expound sutra. After Emperor Qianlong showed the 6th Panchen Lama around the whole temple, he invited the 6th Panchen Lama to give him a sutra lecture. Then, the 6th Panchen Lama dedicated to Emperor Qianlong the records of his prayers and blessings at every stop on his way from Xigaze in Tibet to Chengde.

大红台西边的吉祥法喜殿是六世班禅的寝殿。在这之前，外八庙从未为任何人建过寝宫，这样的特殊待遇，留住了班禅这位宗教首领的心。

Jixiang Faxi Hall (Hall of Joy and Good Luck) on the west side of the Grand Red Hall is the bedroom hall of the 6th Panchen Lama. Before that, there had never been in a sleeping place built for anyone in the Eight Outer Temples, and such special treatment retained the heart of the Panchen Lama the religious leader.

琉璃万寿塔巍踞于须弥福寿之庙中轴线最北的山巅，建在方形基坛上。塔身七层，塔面用绿琉璃砖砌成，镶嵌56尊无量寿佛。

Liuli Wanshou Pagoda (Glazed Pagoda of Longevity), standing on the northernmost peak of the central axis of Xumi Fushou Temple, was built on a square base altar. It is a seven-storey pagoda, made of green glazed bricks, and inlaid with 56 Amitayus Buddhas.

须弥福寿之庙继承了中国古典园林的艺术手法，借助山势起伏，形成错落有致的建筑群，并将植物巧妙地安排其间。在古木与墙面、屋顶的色彩对比中扩展出更悠远的空间。独具匠心的山石丰富着高大建筑的节奏。作为乾隆帝在承德修建的最后一座寺庙，须弥福寿之庙汉藏建筑手法运用自如，中国各民族间文化交流在建筑领域内取得了空前的成就。

Xumi Fushou Temple inherited the artistic techniques of Chinese classical gardens. With the help of the undulating mountains, it formed a well-proportioned group of buildings, among which plants were well arranged, and a more distant space was expanded in the color contrast of the ancient wood and the wall and roof. The unique rocks enriched the rhythm of tall buildings. As the last temple built by Emperor Qianlong in Chengde, Han and Tibetan architectural techniques were applied skillfully in Xumi Fushou Temple, and cultural exchanges among different nationalities in China made unprecedented achievements in the field of architecture.

从溥仁寺到须弥福寿之庙，这些或大或小的庙宇，组团出现在避暑山庄之外，逐步发展为一个享誉中外的寺庙群。当民族合璧交融于建筑，普天同乐合欢于艺术，这些庙宇，也洗去了招抚、怀柔、融合、统一的表情，以庄严华美、渺然尘外的面目示人。

These temples from Puren Temple to Xumi Fushou Temple, large or small, appeared in clusters outside Chengde Mountain Resort and gradually developed into a temple group well-known both at home and abroad. When national integration is reflected in architecture, and the whole world share happiness in art these temples have also washed away the expressions of appeasement, conciliatory, integration and unity, presenting themselves with the solemn, gorgeous appearance.

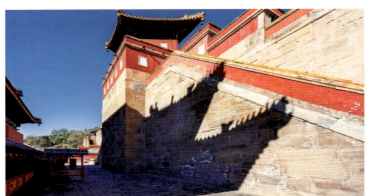

一花一世界，一叶一菩提，每一天的暮鼓晨钟，诉说着曾经的故事，合璧交融、和睦共生。每一处的袅袅香烟，祈求的还是从古到今的不变夙愿："安其居，乐其业，永永普宁。"

To see a world in a flower, and a Bodhi in a leaf. Every day, the evening drum and morning bell in the monastery tell the story of the past, the integration and harmonious coexistence. Incense smoke curls everywhere, praying for the same long-cherished wish from ancient times to the present: "Live cozily; work delightedly; enjoy universal peace for ever."

4

North of the Great River: World Cultural Heritage

The Eastern Royal Tombs of the Qing Dynasty

清东陵

在长达几千年的中国封建社会，作为王朝最高的统治者，很多皇帝一登上龙椅，便开始营建自己的陵墓，地面是现世的权威，地下则是永生的梦想。"事死如事生"，在他们看来，归身之地与现实居所同样重要，他们的丧葬之事自然采用国家的最高礼制来办理。

于是，皇陵这种特殊的建筑，往往凝结了中国人民巧夺天工的艺术才能，收藏着人类文化的瑰宝，体现了当时最高水平的规划思想，集中了那个时代建筑技术和艺术的辉煌成就。

在长达几千年的中国封建社会，作为王朝最高的统治者，很多皇帝一登上龙椅，便开始营建自己的陵墓，地面是现世的权威，地下则是永生的梦想。"事死如事生"，在他们看来，归身之地与现实居所同样重要，他们的丧葬之事自然采用国家的最高礼制来办理。

For thousands of years during Chinese feudal period, as the supreme rulers of dynasty, many emperors started building their own mausoleum as soon as they were enthroned. Above the ground they had authority of the world, and beneath the ground they chased the dream of immortality. "Death is like life". In their eyes, the afterlife resting place was as important as the residence when alive, and their funerals were thus held with the highest ritual standard of the country.

于是，皇陵这种特殊的建筑，往往凝结了中国人民巧夺天工的艺术才能，收藏着人类文化的瑰宝，体现了当时最高水平的规划思想，集中了那个时代建筑技术和艺术的辉煌成就。

Therefore, special constructions such as the imperial mausoleum were built with significant artistic attainment of the Chinese people. It is a valuable collection of human culture which reflects the highest level of construction planning at that time and displays the brilliant achievements of architectural technology and art in that era.

明清是中国陵寝修建史上的集大成时期，将中国古代陵寝的营建推向高峰。明代的明显陵、明孝陵、明十三陵与清代的盛京三陵、清东陵、清西陵一起被列入世界文化遗产名录。

The Ming and the Qing Dynasties were the culminating point of mausoleum construction in Chinese history, pushing the construction of ancient Chinese mausoleums to a peak. The Xianling Tomb, the Xiaoling Tomb, and the Thirteen Tombs of the Ming Dynasty, the Three Tombs in Shengjing, the Eastern Royal Tombs and the Western Royal Tombs of the Qing Dynasty have been listed in the World Cultural Heritage List.

　　盛京三陵地处辽宁。清代入关后修建的两处皇家陵寝都在河北境内，一处在唐山遵化市，一处在保定易县。按照它们相对于北京的方位，遵化的称为东陵，易县的称为西陵。

The Three Tombs in Shengjing were located in Liaoning. The two imperial mausoleums built after the Qing Dynasty entered Shanhaiguan Pass are both in Hebei. One in Zunhua County of Tangshan, and the other in Yixian County of Baoding. According to their direction relative to Beijing, the one in Zunhua is called the Eastern Royal Tombs of the Qing Dynasty, and the one in Yixian is called the Western Royal Tombs of the Qing Dynasty.

　　清东陵的营建早于清西陵，历时247个寒暑。清东陵建有5座皇帝陵、保存有580多座单体建筑，安葬着161名皇室成员，是中国现存规模最为宏大、体系最为完整、保存最为完好的帝王陵墓建筑群。

The construction of the Eastern Royal Tombs of the Qing Dynasty started earlier than that of the Western Royal Tombs of the Qing Dynasty, and it took 247 years to complete. The Eastern Royal Tombs consist of five emperor tombs, more than 580 individual buildings, with 161 members of the royal family buried. This group of tombs are the biggest, the most comprehensive and the best-preserved tombs in China.

在清代之前，唐山遵化还在燕山余脉中沉寂，钟灵毓秀却不为人知。这一带山势不断，气势磅礴，丰台岭卓尔不群。群山环抱之处，是一处开阔的腹地，一马平川，西大河、马兰河映带左右，引来无限情趣和勃勃生机。

Before the Qing Dynasty, Zunhua was little known and remained hidden though endowed with fine spirits of the universe within the Yanshan Mountains. The mountains in this area are continuous and majestic, where the Fengtai Ridge is distinguished. Surrounded by mountains, there is a hinterland, wide and open. With X da River and Malan River on both sides, it arouses much interest and shows great vitality.

公元1651年，一次偶然的邂逅，遵化开始与这个王朝最有权势的一批人联系在了一起，在此后的两百多年岁月里，这里营建活动从未停止，几乎与清王朝相伴始终。

In 1651, by an accidental encounter, Zunhua began to be linked with the most powerful people in the Qing Dynasty. In the following two hundred years, construction activities here never stopped. It almost lasted the entire history of the Qing Dynasty.

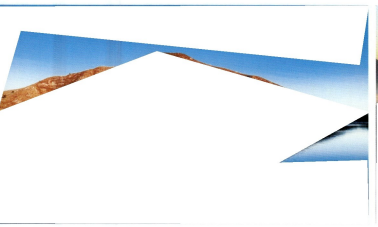

　　这一年，十四岁的顺治帝登顶丰台岭，从山巅远眺，被这一片灵山秀水所震撼，立刻宣布"此山王气葱郁，可为朕寿宫"，并用自己的玉扳指做了标记。

This year, the 14-year-old Emperor Shunzhi climbed to the top of Fengtai Ridge. Looking from the top of the mountain, he was shocked by the marvelous view. He immediately announced, "This mountain resonates with royalty, and it shall be where my mausoleum lies." Shunzhi left his jade thumb ring here as a mark.

　　从后世的文献来看，顺治帝选择这里或许是为了抚慰乡愁。《昌瑞山万年统志》记载，丰台岭"北开幛于雾灵，南列屏于燕壁""含华毓秀，来数千里长白之源"。清帝认为东陵风水所在地为燕山主峰雾灵山，这是由远在数千里之外的长白山逶迤而来，表达了他们认祖归宗的愿望。

From the literature of later generations, Emperor Shunzhi perhaps chose this place because of nostalgia. *Changrui Mountain History Log* records that Fengtai Ridge "starts from Wuling Mountain in the north and stretches along the Yanshan Mountains towards south" "Surrounded with splendid aura of Changbai Mountains from thousands of miles away". The emperor believed that the Fengshui of the Eastern Royal Tombs lies in the Wuling Mountain, originating from Changbai Mountains from far away, which metaphorizes the emperor's respect for ancestors.

在登顶丰台岭十年之后，顺治帝染病宾天。清廷遵其遗愿，在这里开建清代入关后的第一个帝王陵寝——顺治帝的孝陵。作为一代帝王的谢幕之处，丰台岭这个名字显然不够响亮，康熙帝改称为昌瑞山。

Ten years after climbing to the top of Fengtai Ridge, Emperor Shunzhi died of illness. The royal court followed his last wish and built the first emperor's mausoleum the Xiaoling Tomb for Emperor Shunzhi since the Qing Dynasty started and entered Shanhaiguan Pass. As the afterlife resting place for an emperor, the name Fengtai Ridge is apparently not resounding enough. Later, Emperor Kangxi named it Changrui Mountain.

1661年，孝陵开始兴建，它创立了清代皇家陵园的基本规制和美学典范。

In 1661, the construction of the Xiaoling Tomb began. It established the basic standards and aesthetic model for imperial mausoleums in the Qing Dynasty.

西周以前，皇陵不封不树。秦汉时的皇陵，覆斗式封土高大似山陵。唐朝以山为陵，一派大国盛世风貌。元朝实行秘葬，地表无迹可寻。中国古代陵寝的最后辉煌时期出现在明清。明太祖朱元璋创立了一套崭新的陵寝制度，清代承袭了明代陵制，并且注入新的哲学与美学思考。注重周边环境，尽力让建筑与周围的山川形势融为一体，有天人合一的和谐之美；注重建筑形制，每座建筑形体威严庄重，细节烦琐，有种富丽堂皇的宏大之美。

Before the Western Zhou Dynasty, the imperial mausoleums had no mounds or trees grown as marks. When it came to the Qin and Han Dynasties, royal tombs in the flat-top pyramid shape were as tall as mountains. In the Tang Dynasty, mountains were directly used as mausoleums, resonating with the prosperous state under its ruling. The Yuan Dynasty practiced secret burial and left no trace to find on the surface. The last glorious period of ancient Chinese mausoleums appeared in the Ming and the Qing Dynasties. Zhu Yuanzhang the first Emperor of the Ming Dynasty established a new system of mausoleums. The Qing Dynasty inherited the mausoleum system from the Ming Dynasty and infused it with new philosophical and aesthetic ideas: to pay attention to the surroundings and make the building integrate with mountains and rivers, creating a beautiful harmony between man and nature; to pay attention to the architectural form and give each building a majestic and solemn shape with elite details, displaying a beauty of grandeur.

孝陵位于南起金星山，北达昌瑞山主峰的中轴线上，"居中为尊"。十几座建筑被一条约12米宽、5.5千米长的神路连接起来，随着地势起伏，主次分明，井然有序。从高处俯瞰，清东陵路网规整，所有的神路都从孝陵神路上分枝，颇有开枝散叶、百川归海的气势。

　　The Xiaoling Tomb is located on the central axis connecting Jinxing Mountain in the south and the peak of Changrui Mountain in the north. Centered location represents centralized power. More than a dozen landmarks are connected by a 12-meter-wide and 5.5-kilometer-long divine road, well ordered by the ups and downs of terrain. Overlooking from above, the road network of the Eastern Royal Tombs of the Qing Dynasty is neat and tidy. All other divine roads branch off from the Xiaoling Divine Road, as all rivers branch off the sea.

石牌坊是孝陵的第一座建筑，也是孝陵神路的开端。孝陵石牌坊五间六柱十一楼，全部用巨大的青白石构筑而成，这是中国现存面阔最宽的石牌坊。造型宏伟，细节却精巧精致，牌坊各部分饰有不同的石雕，麒麟、狮子、草龙、云龙无不活灵活现。

The stone archway is the first building of Xiaoling Tomb. It is also the start point of the Xiaoling Divine Road. The Xiaoling stone archway consists of five gates, six columns and eleventh roofs, all of which are built with great grey-white marbles. This is the widest stone archway existing in China. The shape is magnificent, and the details are exquisite. Each part of the archway is decorated with vivid stone carvings: kylins, lions, grass dragons and cloud- dragons.

牌坊后的大红门，是孝陵的大门，也是整个清东陵的总门户，左右原本建有延绵20里的风水墙，如同两条臂膀护卫着整个陵园。可惜几经沧桑，现存风水墙已不足1000米。

The big red gate behind the archway is the gate of Xiaoling Tomb and it is also the gate of the entire Eastern Royal Tombs. There used to be a ten-kilometer long Fengshui wall on both sides, like two arms guarding the entire cemetery. It is a pity that after ages of vicissitudes, the existing Fengshui wall is less than one kilometer in total.

大红门是一座面阔38米的单檐庑殿顶建筑，有三个拱券式门洞。门，在中国封建社会中被赋予多重意义，在这里代表着国家的礼法。左为君门，皇帝通行；右为臣门，大臣通行；中为神门，帝后棺椁和神牌通行。

The big red gate is a 38-meter wide single-eave hip-roof building with three arched gates. Gates were endowed with multiple meanings in Chinese feudal society, representing the nation's etiquette. The gate on the left was for the emperor; the gate on the right was for ministers; the gate in the middle was for royal coffins of emperors and queens, along with their spirit tablets to pass.

虽然礼制如此安排，但实际上从这道大门建成之日起，就从来没有棺椁从神门通过。建造者或许低估了帝后葬礼的排场，每个棺椁有128人托抬。128位杠夫加上巨大的棺椁，显然无法通过不足6米宽的神门。救急的往往是旁边的风水墙，拆掉一段来应急，事后再做修复。

Although the ritual system was arranged in this way, in fact, since the gate was built, no coffin ever passed through the middle gate. The builders might have underestimated the scale of royal funerals. Each royal coffin was carried by 128 men. With 128 carriers plus the giant coffin itself, it was obvious that they could not pass through the middle gate which was less than 6 meters in width. Thus, on such an occasion, part of the Fengshui wall was torn down for emergency use, and then got repaired afterwards.

这道好似派不上用场的大红门，却隐藏着建造者的精妙构思。站在大红门南30米处，透过三个门洞向北看，门洞有如相机的取景框，将大碑楼巧妙地定格在构图之中。在大红门北30米处向南看，金星山、石牌坊也分别入画。

This seemingly useless big red gate actually concealed the designer's subtle ideas. Standing 30 meters to the south of the gate and looking towards north through the three arched gates, the gate is like a camera's viewfinder, which skillfully draw a picture of the Dabei Building. Looking south 30 meters north of the big red gate, Jinxing Mountain and the stone archway are also included in the view.

大清江北
世界文化遗产

　　这是中国古代建筑中建筑间距的一种处理手法，过白。靠着巧妙的距离选择，使得门框、门洞如同画框，将景物剪裁、镶框，蕴含着中国古建独有的意境之美。这种"框景"的艺术手法，几乎在东陵所有过门、券洞、梁枋处都有运用。熟悉的景色换个观察角度重新出现，肃穆中有灵动，宏大中见雅致。

　　This is a way of dealing with the spacing between buildings in ancient Chinese architecture, which is called "guobai". The clever choice of distance makes the door frame and door opening function as picture frames. The framed scenery contains the unique beauty of Chinese ancient architecture. This kind of artistic technique of "framed scene" is used in almost all gates in the Eastern Royal Tombs. When the same scenery reappears from a different angle, there is agility in solemnity and elegance in grandeur.

　　大碑楼的核心要素自然是"碑"，碑文记载着逝者的功绩，寄托着后人的哀思。碑一般有两种，神功圣德碑和圣德神功碑，开国的君王立碑为神功圣德碑，之后的帝王立碑为圣德神功碑。碑文由后继者书写，分满、汉两种文字镌刻。

　　The core element of the Dabei Building is stele. The inscription on the stele records the achievements of the deceased and sustains the condolences of future generations. There are generally two types of steles: the stele of divine achievement with holy virtue and the stele of holy virtue with divine achievement. The former was for the first emperor who established the dynasty and the latter was for the successors of the throne. The inscription on the stele was written by the successor and it was engraved in both Manchu and Han.

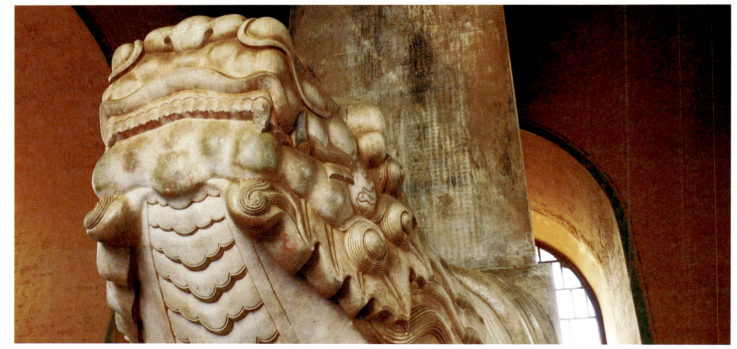

孝陵神路，因势随形，直中见曲。石像生的出现，为神路平添了几分威严。石像生南北行进870米，文臣、武将与各种瑞兽构成一组威武雄壮的仪卫。这是清代皇陵中规模最大的一组石像生。这十八对石雕像均以整块石料雕成，朴拙粗犷，形神兼备。

The Xiaoling Divine Road was built along with the shape of terrain, heading straight with some detours in between. The appearance of the stone statues added an element of majesty to this road. The stone statues lining up 870 meters from north to south, consist of civil servants, military generals and various auspicious animals, which formed a group of mighty and majestic guards. This is the largest group of stone statues in the imperial tombs of the Qing Dynasty. The 18 pairs of stone statues are each carved from a single piece of stone, simple and robust, both in form and spirit.

清东陵
The Eastern Royal Tombs of the Qing Dynasty | 197

在陵墓前设置石像生的做法起源于东汉，后世沿用不衰。据说为了节约，康熙帝取消了这一规制。乾隆帝建陵时，又将此例恢复，给诸位先祖补立了石像生。

The practice of setting up stone statues in front of the mausoleum originated in the Eastern Han Dynasty, and it continued to be used in later generations. It is said that in order to minimize cost, Emperor Kangxi abolished this regulation. But when Emperor Qianlong was building his mausoleum, he restored this practice, made up and built stone statues for the ancestors.

石像生的两旁，植有一大片柏树。据说，古时有一种名叫魍象的怪物，嗜食死人肝脑，但害怕老虎和柏树。因此人们常在墓地安放石雕老虎、种植柏树以驱赶魍象，演变日久而成为建陵规制。

On both sides of the stone statues, lots of cypresses are planted. It is said that in ancient times there was a monster called the "Wang Xiang", which loved to eat the liver and brain of the dead, but was afraid of tigers and cypresses. Therefore, people often placed stone-carved tigers in the cemetery and planted cypresses to drive away the monster. By and by, this became the rules for building mausoleums.

　　孝陵建有东陵唯一的一座龙凤门。三座大门由青白石柱和额枋组成。柱子顶端蹲踞着一只望天犼。石座之上建有一段琉璃影壁。不管是线条还是颜色，石像生与龙凤门对比强烈，丰富着视觉的层次。

　　Only the Xiaoling Tomb has the dragon and phoenix gate in the Eastern Royal Tombs. The three gates are composed of grey-white marble pillars and headings. On the top of the pillar squats a sky-watching hound. Between each two archways there is a glazed painted wall. The contrast on the lining and color between the stone statues and gates is strong, enriching the visual impact.

　　四座桥之后，才是孝陵的主体宫殿区。宫殿区一如皇宫，是前朝后寝的布局。经过神道碑亭、东西朝房，从隆恩门进入陵院。陵院的主体是隆恩殿，也称享殿，是陵寝地面上最主要的建筑。逝者牌位在这里供奉，大的祭礼活动也在这里举行。

　　After four bridges is the main palace area of the Xiaoling Tomb. The palace area in the mausoleum is just like the real royal palace, suggesting the ruling power in the afterlife. After passing through the divine stele pavilion and the horizontally facing rooms, one enters the mausoleum from Long'en Gate. The main body of the mausoleum is the Long'en Palace, also known as the Hall of Enjoyment, which is the most important building on the ground in the mausoleum. The memorial tablets of the deceased were enshrined here and large ceremonies were also held here.

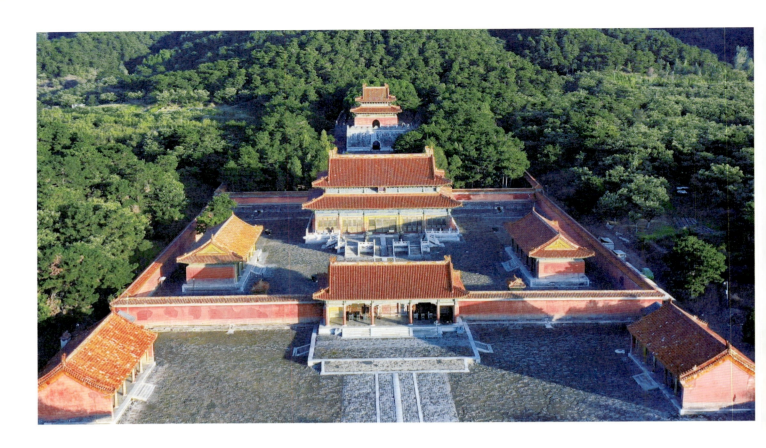

陵寝门后便是第二道陵院，门后的二柱门是礼制性建筑，只有皇帝陵才会有。后来，道光帝裁撤了它，慕陵之后的陵园里再也没有了它的身影。陵院最高的建筑是明楼，建在方城台面正中。宝城护卫着宝顶，宝顶下是顺治帝的地宫，也就是他最后的葬身之处。

Behind the Lingqin Gate is the second mausoleum. The two-pillar gate behind the gate is a ritual architecture, which was exclusive to the royal mausoleum. Later, Emperor Daoguang abolished it and it was no longer seen in the cemetery after the Muling Tomb. The tallest landmark in the mausoleum is the Minglou Building which was built in the center of the square city castle. The castle guards the sacred building and below the building lies the palace of Emperor Shunzhi—his final burial place.

孝陵确立了后世陵寝的建筑规制、秩序与礼制，宫殿建筑"前朝后寝"的体制和"前方后圆"的布局，以明确的轴线，组织成既相互独立，又传承有序、隶属明确的建筑群。

The Xiaoling Tomb established the architectural style, regulation and ritual system of the mausoleums for later generations. The system of "front as court and back as residence" and the layout of "front being square and rear being circle" of the palace building were organized with a clear axis to connect all landmarks neatly and orderly while maintaining each of their uniqueness.

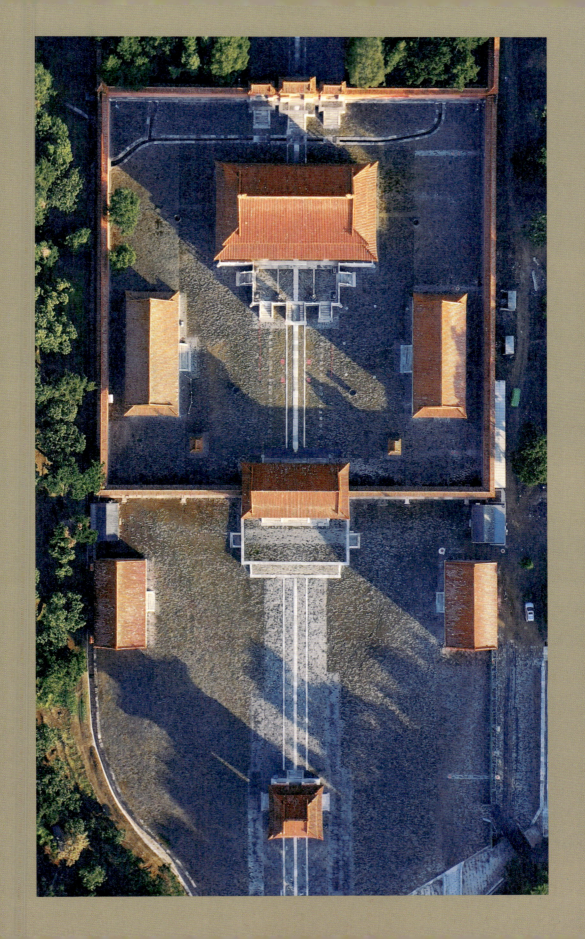

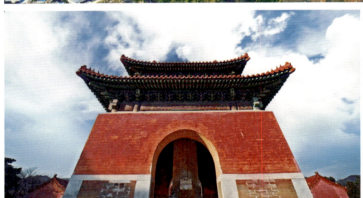

在清祖陵永陵里，有并排而立的四祖碑楼，建筑样式和规模大小完全相同。入关之后，在以汉文化主导的东陵里，建筑体量与规模因辈分而区别明显。东陵以孝陵为中心，其余陵寝众星拱月。

In the Yongling Tomb of the ancestors of the Qing Dynasty, there are four stele buildings standing side by side, with the exact same architectural style and scale. Since the beginning of the Qing Dynasty, in the Eastern Royal Tombs, which was dominated by Han culture, the building volume and scale were obviously differentiated by seniority. In the Eastern Royal Tombs, the Xiaoling Tomb was located in the center, surrounded by all other royal tombs in the cemetery.

孝陵的美学典范被后继者承袭。建筑的组合与搭配极其讲究，建筑物的大小、高低、远近、疏密皆以"百尺为形，千尺为势"的尺度进行视觉控制，同时将山川形胜纳于景框之中，作为建筑的对景、底景和衬景。孝陵之美，在于单体建筑所凝结的精致之美，在于森严秩序所传达出的宏伟之美，更在于山川形胜与陵寝建筑"天人合一"的和谐大美。

The aesthetics of the Xiaoling Tomb was inherited by successors. The combination and collocation of buildings were very considerate. The size, height, distance and density of buildings were all visually controlled, "A hundred feet to determine the shape and a thousand feet to see landscape." It combined the mountains to the building's backgrounds to build contrasting or resonating sceneries. From the exquisite beauty condensed by each building, the aesthetics of the Xiaoling Tomb reflected the grand beauty conveyed by the orderly layout, and the harmonious beauty combining man and nature between the mausoleum buildings and the view of mountains and rivers.

孝陵东侧一千米处的是康熙帝的景陵，这是东陵的第二座皇帝陵。

One thousand meters on the east of the Xiaoling Tomb is the Jingling Tomb of Emperor Kangxi, which is the second emperor's mausoleum in the Eastern Royal Tombs.

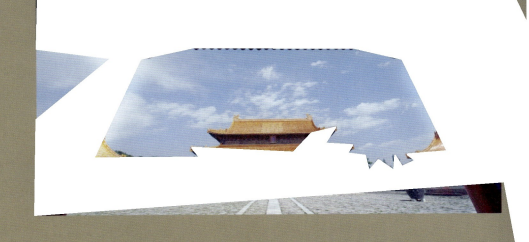

康熙帝八岁即位，十四岁亲政，擒鳌拜、定三藩，抗击沙俄，统一台湾，征服准噶尔，创立多伦会盟。在位六十一年的康熙帝，开启了中国封建社会最后一个盛世——康乾盛世。

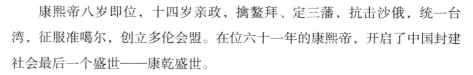

Emperor Kangxi ascended the throne at the age of eight, and took charge of the government at the age of fourteen. Through crushing the coup of high-level minister Ao Bai, suppressing three rebel forces, fighting against the invasion of Tsarist Russia, taking back Taiwan, conquering Dzungaria and establishing Duolun Commission to rule over Mongol, Emperor Kangxi, who reigned for 61 years, opened the last prosperous age of Chinese feudal society—the Kang-Qian Flourishing Age.

雍正帝十分崇拜自己的父亲，亲自撰写了景陵圣德神功碑的碑文，四千三百多字的文章足以刻满一块石碑。雍正帝做主将父亲的圣德神功碑多加了一块，东碑刻满文，西碑为汉文，景陵首创双碑之后，雍正帝的泰陵、乾隆帝的裕陵、嘉庆帝的昌陵，都效仿景陵，功德碑均立双碑。

Emperor Yongzheng admired his father Emperor Kangxi very much and wrote the inscription on Jingling Tomb's stele of holy virtue with divine achievement by himself. The more than 4,300 words were enough for one piece of stele. Therefore, Emperor Yongzheng ordered an additional stele for his father. The east stele was inscribed in Manchu and the west stele was in Chinese. After Jingling Tomb created the first double-stele tradition, Emperor Yongzheng's Tailing Tomb, Emperor Qianlong's Yuling Tomb, and Emperor Jiaqing's Changling Tomb all followed the example of Jingling Tomb and used double steles.

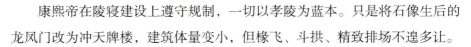

康熙帝在陵寝建设上遵守规制，一切以孝陵为蓝本。只是将石像生后的龙凤门改为冲天牌楼，建筑体量变小，但椽飞、斗拱、精致排场不遑多让。

Emperor Kangxi followed the construction traditions inherited from ancestors and built mausoleums based on the Xiaoling Tomb. Only the dragon and phoenix gate was changed to a towering archway. The building volume decreased, but the exquisite rafters, arches and overall style were not lost.

雍正帝择吉壤时出了点小问题，权衡之下，在保定易县另辟陵地。为了不使先祖寂寞，乾隆帝开创"父东子西，父西子东"的"昭穆相间的兆葬之制"。循着制度，在东陵为自己开建裕陵。

　　There was a small complication when Emperor Yongzheng chose the auspicious land for his tomb. After consideration, he set up another mausoleum in Yixian County of Baoding. In order to accompany ancestors, Emperor Qianlong created the burial system of "Zhao Mu". When the father was buried in the east, the son was to be buried in the west, and vice versa. Following the system, Emperor Qianlong built Yuling Tomb for himself in the Eastern Royal Tombs.

　　乾隆时期，经济发展、文化繁荣。强盛的国力，也显示在裕陵的修建上，裕陵费时九年，耗银203万两。

　　During Emperor Qianlong's reign, both economy and culture were flourishing. The strong national strength is also shown in the construction of Yuling Tomb, which cost 2.03 million taels of silver and lasted nine years.

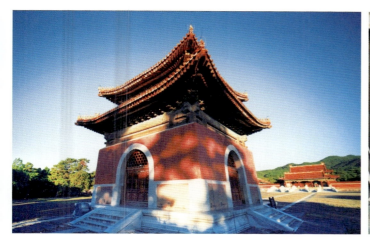

　　从表面上看，所有建筑都在规制内，但工精料美，材料、细节都下足了功夫。所用石料毫不迁就，主体建筑的阶条石均为整块石料，使用最多的艾叶青石，质地坚固，可与汉白玉媲美。

　　Superficially, all buildings were within the traditional royal regulations, but the workmanship was exquisite, and the materials and details were well crafted. The stone materials used were luxurious, as each main building's step stone was an entire piece of stone. And the most-used folium grey-white stone was solid and comparable to white marble.

裕陵隆恩殿后、陵寝门前的玉带河上，增置了三座玉带桥。桥孔用青白石拱券而成，券脸上端有吸水兽，桥面两侧安装白石栏杆，龙凤柱头，造型优美，雕刻精细，与其他帝陵的平桥相比，隆重了不少。

　　Inside the Yuling Tomb, between Long'en Palace and Mausoleum gate, three jade belt bridges were added on the jade belt river. The aperture of the bridge was made of grey-white marble to support the arch, with a guarding animal "Xishuishou" statue on the top. White stone railings were installed on both sides of the bridge deck along with dragon and phoenix pillars. The aesthetic style and exquisite carving craft made the mausoleum stand out from others which only use flat-designed bridges.

　　最奢华的是裕陵的地宫，耗时三年建成。进入地宫仿佛走入另一个世界，既是精美的石雕艺术宝库，也是肃穆的地下佛堂。

　　The most luxurious part was the underground palace of the Yuling Tomb, which took three years to build. The underground palace was like a different world. It was not only a treasure house of exquisite stone carving art, but also a solemn underground Buddhist hall.

地宫规模不大，进深54米，面积372平方米，平面呈"主"字形，由九券四门构成。"券"是指墓室中顶部呈拱式的建筑，九券最为隆重，帝后的棺椁放在最深处的金券内，要想进入，必须打开四道石门。

The underground palace was compact in scale, with a depth of 54 meters and overall area of 372 square meters. The layout looked like the Chinese character "主" from above, and the palace consist of nine Quans and four gates. "Quan" refers to the building with an arched top in the tomb, and nine Quans suggested the highest solemnity. The coffins of the emperors and queens were placed in the deepest golden Quan. To enter it, one must open all four stone gates.

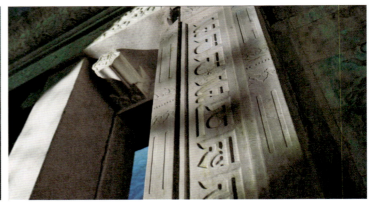

除了第四道石门没有门楼之外，其余三座石门的门楼都用整块石料雕成，脊吻、走兽栩栩如生，佛像、法器惟妙惟肖。两旁门垛上刻有梵文咒语，门垛下部雕饰成须弥座样式。四道石门由整块青白玉石打磨而成，八个门扇，分别雕刻一尊菩萨立像，每尊菩萨像高约1.5米，体态婀娜，神情柔和安详，尽显佛家的静谧与平和。

Except for the fourth stone gate, which had no gatehouse, the gatehouses of the other three stone gates were all carved from a single piece of stone, with vivid animals and Buddhist statutes. There were Sanskrit mantras engraved on the gate frames on both sides, and the lower part of the gate frame was carved in the style of Sumero seat. The four stone gates were polished from a whole piece of grey-white jade stone. The eight door leaves were each carved with a standing Bodhisattva statue. Each Bodhisattva statue was about 1.5 meters tall, with various gestures and harmonious faces, suggesting zen and peace in Buddhism.

　　门洞券里雕刻着四大天王坐像，大小与真人相仿，横眉立目，魁梧伟岸。穿堂券两侧雕刻着"五欲供图"，五座器座之上各生莲花一组，分别托承五种佛前的供养品，对应的是色、声、香、味、触五欲。明堂券顶雕刻有"五方佛"，五方佛占据东西南北中五个方位，各显神通，各具智慧。金券是主墓室，佛花、佛像、八宝花纹刻满了整个墓室。

　　Inside the gates were the Four Heavenly Kings on the wall engravings. The real-person-sized statues had frowned eyebrows and strong physical postures. On both sides of the wall was engraved with "Five Desires". Each of the five pedestals had a set of lotus blossoms, which held five kinds of offerings in front of the Buddha, corresponding to the five desires of vision, sound, smell, taste and touch. The ceiling of the Mingtang Quan was engraved with "Five-Direction Buddhas", expressing holiness and wisdom. The golden Quan was the main tomb and it was engraved with Buddhist blossoms and statues, along with eight-treasure patterns.

墓道石门高3米、宽1.5米，重达3000千克。葬礼完毕，各道石门封死，永世不启。

The stone gate of the tomb is 3 meters high, 1.5 meters wide, and weighs 3,000 kilograms. After the funeral was completed, all stone gates were sealed and never to be opened.

1928年7月，军阀孙殿英部队以军事演习为名，在东陵开始有计划的盗墓行动。裕陵地宫壁垒森严、牢不可破的石门，被炸药破开，地宫里的珍宝被洗劫一空，大部分至今下落不明。

In July 1928, Sun Dianying a warlord initiated planned tomb raiding operation in the Eastern Royal Tombs of the Qing Dynasty in the name of military drill. The fortified and unbreakable stone gate of the Yuling Tomb's underground palace was destroyed with explosives. All the treasures in the underground palace were looted, most of which are still missing.

然而，在这场浩劫中有一样珍品却依然保留了下来。整个裕陵地宫雕刻有三万多字藏文-梵文的佛经咒语，这些阴刻的经文，雕刻刀法遒劲，布局得体，字体隽秀。今天，在学者专家孜孜不倦地解读下，这些深埋地下的瑰宝穿透岁月的隧道，重新绽放出文化的光彩。

However, there is one treasure that survived this catastrophe. The entire underground palace of the Yuling Tomb was engraved with more than 30,000 characters of Buddhist scriptures and mantras in Tibetan and Sanskrit. These inscribed scriptures were carved with impeccable carving skills, decent layout and beautiful fonts. Today, thanks to the sedulous translation work done by scholars and experts, these treasures buried deep in the ground have traveled through time and now re-bloom the brilliance of culture.

清中后期，国力衰弱，咸丰帝的定陵与同治帝的惠陵渐显颓势。修建定陵时，恰逢第二次鸦片战争战败赔款，国库空虚，不得已选用了宝华峪道光帝弃陵的大量旧料。

In the middle and late Qing Dynasty, the national strength was weakened. Emperor Xianfeng's Dingling Tomb and Emperor Tongzhi's Huiling Tomb gradually declined in scale. The Dingling Tomb was built right after the defeat and reparation of the Second Opium War, and the national treasury was in fiscal deficit. Therefore, a great amount of former abandoned materials from the mausoleum of Emperor Daoguang in Baohua Valley were used as a last resort.

好在主持修造定陵与惠陵的建筑师是雷思起，虽说材料简陋，施工匆忙，还是靠着过硬的专业能力维持了一定的水准，尤其是定陵，建筑层层叠落，韵律感十足，形成跌宕起伏的豪华气势。

Fortunately, the architect who presided over the construction of the Dingling Tomb and the Huiling Tomb was Lei Siqi. Although the materials were simple and the construction was built in a hurry, he still maintained a decent level with his excellent professional ability, especially the Dingling Tomb, where buildings were layered and rhythmic, forming a luxury sense of depth.

雷思起是清代建筑修建传奇家族"样式雷"的第六代传人，在两百多年时间里，雷氏家族有七代人担任清代皇家建筑设计机构——样式房的总设计师，"样式雷"成为雷氏家族的金字招牌。雷氏家族设计修建了大量最高等级的皇家建筑，故宫、天坛、颐和园、避暑山庄等均被列入世界文化遗产名录，"样式雷"创造了许多古建筑史上的奇迹。

Lei Siqi was the sixth-generation descendant of the legendary architectural family "Style Lei" in the Qing Dynasty. In the past two hundred years, seven generations of the Lei family served as the chief designer of royal architectures for the Qing Dynasty. "Style Lei" became the golden signature of the Lei family. The Lei family designed and built a large number of the highest-level royal buildings. The Forbidden City, the Temple of Heaven, the Summer Palace, and Chengde Mountain Resort have all been included in the World Cultural Heritage List. "Style Lei" has created many miracles in the history of ancient architecture.

慈禧与慈安的定东陵也由雷思起主持修建，留下了东陵建造史上的又一个传奇。

The Dingdong Tombs of Empress Dowager Cixi and Empress Dowager Ci'an were also built by Lei Siqi, leaving another legend in the history of the construction of the Eastern Royal Tombs.

　　雷思起设计两座定东陵时可谓步步惊心，波澜不断。为了平衡两宫太后的高低尊卑，他数易其稿，费尽心力，终于拿出一个万全的方案。他突破既有皇后陵的规制，设计建造了两座规模大小、风格完全相同的皇后陵。在雷思起看来，这个方案集合了清朝历代皇后陵的建筑特色，各类建筑设施一应俱全，还破天荒设计了"凤压龙"丹陛石，可以说，他竭尽全力，触到了规制的天花板。

　　When Lei Siqi was designing the two Dingdong Tombs, he encountered many complications. In order to balance the superiority between the two empress dowagers of the two palaces, he spent a long time working on the draft and finally came up with a perfect plan. He surpassed the existing regulations for Queen's mausoleum and built two royal tombs of the same size and style. In Lei Siqi's opinion, this plan combined all the architectural features of the tombs of the empresses during the Qing Dynasty. And he used an unprecedented design of the "Phoenix above Dragon" Danbi Stone. One can say that Lei Siqi tried his best and for sure reached the ceiling of royal regulations.

　　不知是承受了太多的压力还是投入了太多的精力，定东陵让雷思起耗尽心血，因劳瘁而去世。雷思起无从知道，他呕心沥血的万全之策并未得到慈禧的完全认可。慈安去世后，慈禧独揽大权。为了体现身份和地位，她下令将当初耗银227万两建好的陵墓全部重新修缮。

　　Perhaps it was because of the high pressure and long working hours, Lei Siqi died of exhaustion after building the Dingdong Tombs. However, Lei Siqi would never know that his painstaking effort was not fully recognized by Empress Dowager Cixi. After Empress Dowager Ci'an's death, Cixi owned exclusive power. In order to show her superior status, she ordered the tomb that was built at a cost of 2.27 million taels of silver to be renovated.

　　慈禧重修陵寝所耗银两中，大量挪用了清廷的海军军饷。重修后的慈禧陵，用料之讲究，做工之精细，装修之豪华，建筑之精美，使与之毗邻的慈安陵为之逊色。慈禧陵据说有"三绝"，木绝、金绝和石绝。

　　Among the money spent on the renovation, Empress Dowager Cixi also embezzled a large amount from the national naval force's salaries. The renovated Cixi Tomb was exquisite in workmanship and architecture, luxurious in materials and decoration, making the adjacent Ci'an Tomb inferior to it. Cixi Tomb was said to have "three uniques" in wood, gold and stone.

　　"木绝"是说隆恩殿与东西配殿的梁、枋都是用木中非常名贵稀有的黄花梨木制成，上品黄花梨木木质坚硬，纹理细密，寸木寸金。

　　Unique in wood means that the beams and frames of the Long'en Palace and the east and west side halls were all made of very precious and rare huanghuali wood.

　　"金绝"，三大殿的梁枋彩画不做地仗，不敷颜料，而在木件上直接沥粉贴金，图案为等级最高的金龙和玺彩画。64根露明柱子上全部盘绕半立体的镀金铜龙。墙上寓意"万福万寿、福寿绵长"的五蝠捧寿、万（卍）字不到头图案等，也全都筛扫黄金。据清宫档案记载，仅三大殿所用的叶子金就达4592两之多。

　　Unique in gold means the color paintings on the beams and frames of the three palaces did not use pigments as primer, but directly plastered with gold on the wood pieces, drawing the highest-level color painting called Gold Dragon and Royal Seal. The 64 Luming pillars were all coiled with gold-plated bronze dragons. On the wall, the Wufu Pengshou pattern (five bats holding longevity peaches) and endless swastika character suggesting ultimate blessing and longevity were also sifted out of gold. According to the records left by the Qing Dynasty, just the three major palaces alone cost 4,592 taels of leaf gold.

　　"石绝"，石料一律采用上好的汉白玉，石雕图案更是绝中之绝，凤压着龙。在中国封建社会，纲常伦理为重中之重，夫为妻纲，尊卑有序，不能僭越。唯一例外的就是权力。

　　Unique in stone suggests that all stone materials were made of high-quality white marble. And the stone carving patterns were one of a kind, putting the phoenix above the dragon. In Chinese feudal society, he ethics always required wives to follow their husbands. Superiority was strictly ordered and could not be overstepped, but the only exception was power.

这是慈禧主政的时代，各式龙凤呈祥图案也都随之改动，凤为主导，龙为从属。殿前的丹陛石，丹凤凌空、蛟龙出水。76根望柱，翔凤雄踞柱头，盘龙雕在柱身，"一凤压两龙"造型。汉白玉栏板雕刻图案"凤引龙追"。

　　This is the era of Empress Dowager Cixi, and all the old patterns of dragon and phoenix were changed into phoenix being the dominant and the dragon being the subordinate. In the carvings on the Danbi stone before the Palace, phoenix flies into the sky and dragons jump out of the water. Among the 76 pillars, auspicious phoenix is at the head of the pillar, and the dragons are carved on the pillar body, forming an image of "one phoenix above two dragons". And the engraved pattern on the white marble balustrade shows "phoenix leads and dragons chase."

慈禧地宫的随葬品更是奢华异常，据李莲英侄子写的《爱月轩笔记》记载，仅往棺内填空的珍珠与宝石就价值223万两白银。

　　The burial objects in Cixi's underground palace were even more extravagant. According to the *Notes of Aiyuexuan* written by Li Lianying's nephew, the pearls and gems that filled in the coffin alone were worth 2.23 million taels of silver.

生前追求极致奢华的慈禧并未料到，军阀孙殿英会用火药炸开这座被她倾国力打造的"万年吉壤"。那些曾经为她带来殊荣、给她安慰的奇珍异宝最终离她而去。这场劫难距离她下葬仅仅只隔了十九年时间。

Cixi, who pursued the ultimate luxury during her lifetime, did not expect that the warlord Sun Dianying would use gunpowder to blow up this "auspicious soil for centuries" that took a nation's strength to build. Those rare treasures that had brought her honor and comfort had finally left her. This catastrophe happened only nineteen years after her burial.

盗墓者的炮火击碎了帝王追求的所谓永恒，也湮灭了一个没落王朝的背影。风云散尽后，恢宏的建筑依然挺立在山水间，静静地倾听着历史的足音。

The cannon fire of the tomb raiders shattered the so-called eternity dream pursued by emperors and annihilated the shadow of a declining dynasty. After ups and downs, the magnificent buildings still stand between the mountains and rivers, quietly listening to the footsteps of history.

曾经澎湃的万顷松涛，如今成为丰收在望的果园。漫步其间的不再是守卫皇陵的卫兵，取而代之的是自在生长的生灵。而那些曾经的守卫者，也在变动的岁月中开启了新的生活。有些敞开了家园，迎接着四面八方前来访古的游人，讲述着一些渐渐被遗忘的往事。有些守护着古老的工艺，在日复一日的雕琢中，挽留着曾经的美丽。清东陵，这个记录着三百年沧桑的地方，在建筑与自然"天人合一"之后，也找到自己与人最佳的相处方式。

The place used to be worshipped by the world has now become an orchard expecting harvest. The guards guarding the imperial mausoleum who used to roam inside are now replaced by living creatures that grow freely. And those former guardians also started a new life in the changing years. Some have opened their homes to welcome tourists from all over the world, telling stories of the forgotten past. Some guard the ancient craftsmanship and retain the beauty of the past in the day-to-day carving, The Eastern Royal Tombs of the Qing Dynasty, a place that recorded the vicissitudes of three hundred years finally found the harmony to get along with man and nature.

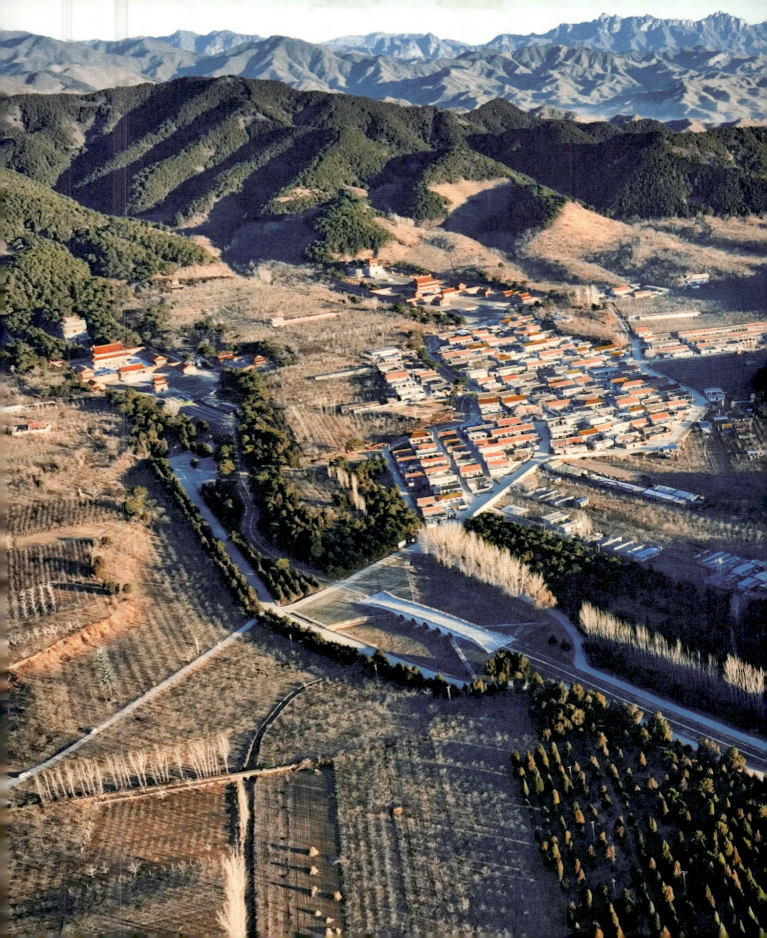

5 清西陵

North of the Great River: World Cultural Heritage

The Western Royal Tombs of the Qing Dynasty

在河北易县，永宁山下，易水河畔有一片八百平方公里的谷地，高山、丘陵、平原、河流等地貌齐全，天造地设，万物和谐。半闭合的自然环境，正是古人所追求的"天人合一"的理想居所，被清代风水大师誉为"乾坤聚秀之区，阴阳会合之所"。

这里便是清王朝最后的万年吉壤。从1730年到1915年，185年间，在方圆83平方千米的范围内，清西陵相继建成了4座皇帝陵、3座皇后陵、14座皇家陵寝、一座行宫、一座皇家寺庙永福寺、数处营房和衙署等配套建筑，是现存陵寝建筑类型最为齐全的中国古代皇家陵墓群。

在古人的观念里，皇帝陵寝的修建是事关国祚绵长、政局稳定、人心安定的国之要典。自古以来，历代帝王总是在刚登基时就着手寻找万年吉壤来营造自己的身后世界，以期这块风水宝地能给继承者以及江山社稷带来好运。

In the concept of the ancients, the construction of the emperor's mausoleum was an important matter of the country, which was related to the longevity of the country, stability of the political situation, and stability of public feeling. Since ancient times, the emperors had always set out to find auspicious land for mausoleums as soon as they ascended the throne to start building their royal world for the afterlife, hoping this auspicious land would bring good luck to successors and the nation.

在河北易县，永宁山下，易水河畔有一片800平方千米的谷地，高山、丘陵、平原、河流等地貌齐全，天造地设，万物和谐。半闭合的自然环境，正是古人所追求的"天人合一"的理想居所，被清代风水大师誉为"乾坤聚秀之区，阴阳会合之所"。

In Yixian County of Hebei Province, at the foot of the Yongning Mountain, there is a valley of 800 square kilometers along Yishui River, covering many land forms such as mountains, hills, plains and rivers. The semi-covered natural environment is the ideal place for the "harmony between man and nature" pursued by the ancients. It is praised by the Fengshui masters of Qing Dynasty as "the area where the universe gathers and the place where Yin and Yang meet".

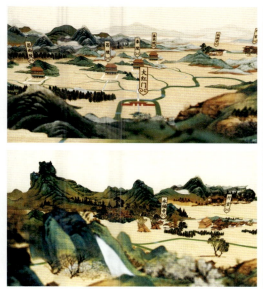

这里便是清王朝最后的万年吉壤。从1730年到1915年，185年间，在方圆83平方千米的范围内，清西陵相继建成了四座皇帝陵、三座皇后陵、十四座皇家陵寝、一座行宫、一座皇家寺庙永福寺、数处营房和衙署等配套建筑，是现存陵寝建筑类型最为齐全的中国古代皇家陵墓群。

This is the last auspicious land of the Qing Dynasty. From 1730 to 1915, during 185 years, within a radius of 83 square kilometers, inside the Western Royal Tombs of the Qing Dynasty, the royal family built four emperor mausoleums, three empress mausoleums, fourteen royal mausoleums, one resort palace, one royal temple—the Yongfu Temple, and several imperial institutions, making Western Royal Tombs the most comprehensive tombs existing to include so many types of constructions.

这也是中国封建王朝的最后一处帝王陵墓群，荣耀与衰亡的关联，亲情与权位的纠缠，如今都已凝固在山水之间。一个曾经煊赫的王朝，一代代的皇权更迭，最终在这里尘埃落定。

This is also the last imperial mausoleum group from the feudal dynasty period in China. Glory and falls, family affections and the game of thrones have all been buried in the mountains and rivers. A once prosperous dynasty along with the transition of power for generations finally settled here.

清西陵行宫门口是一片茂密的松树，初秋的阳光下，树木生机勃发。一百多年前，这里曾经是一座火车站，从这里延伸出去一条长40多千米的铁路——高易铁路，转乘后可通往北京。

In front of the Xinggong Palace of the Western Royal Tombs is a dense field of pine trees, full of vitality. More than 100 years ago, here it used to be a railway station. From here, the Gaoyi Railway stretched across more than 40 kilometers and could commute all the way to Beijing with transfers.

这是中国人自行设计和建造的第一条铁路，它的总工程师就是赫赫有名的詹天佑。1903年4月5日，这条铁路首次通车，搭载的客人是当时王朝的最高统治者慈禧与光绪帝，他们乘车的目的是谒陵。相比以往至少三四天的车马劳顿，几个小时车程的火车确实是当时最舒服的选择。

This is the first railway designed and built by Chinese people, and its chief engineer is the famous Zhan Tianyou. On April 5, 1903, the railway was put into use and the first passengers were Empress Dowager Cixi and Emperor Guangxu the supreme rulers of the dynasty. They were on their way to visit the imperial mausoleum and pay their respects. Compared with sitting on a horse wagon that took at least three to four days, a train ride for a few hours was indeed the most comfortable choice at that time.

从北京出发，到易县的西陵是125千米，到遵化的东陵也是125千米。两百多年前，这个巧合也给特立独行、坚持选择这里为吉壤的雍正帝增添了些许信心。

From Beijing, it is 125 kilometers to the Western Royal Tombs in Yixian County and also 125 kilometers to the Eastern Royal Tombs in Zunhua. More than two hundred years ago, this coincidence also provided confidence to Emperor Yongzheng, who was stubborn enough to choose this place as the auspicious land.

公元1729年，即位七年的雍正帝突然命人寻找建陵的吉壤。按常理来说，这个时间晚了一些，大部分皇帝都是一登基即勘穴建陵。后续的事情更出乎意料，大臣受命勘测，多次在东陵占卜选择，均未找到相宜之处。

In 1729, Emperor Yongzheng, who had been on the throne for seven years, suddenly ordered people to find an auspicious land to build his tomb. According to traditions, the timing was a little bit late, as most emperors usually started the searching work as soon as they ascended to the throne. The ministers who were appointed to the searching mission made many divinations within the Eastern Royal Tombs but could not find an appropriate place.

清西陵
The Western Royal Tombs of the Qing Dynasty | **233**

　　很快，洞悉圣心的怡亲王声称在易县境内泰宁山天平峪发现了风水宝地。这里风景秀美自然不用多说，单"泰宁山、天平峪"这两个听起来低调却寓意祥和的地名，就切中了雍正帝的心意。

Soon, Emperor Yongzheng's brother Prince Yi reported to have discovered an auspicious land in Tianping Valley in Taining Mountain in Yixian County. The two names "Taining Mountain and Tianping Valley" imply peace and blessing, which pleased Emperor Yongzheng.

　　之后更名为永宁山的泰宁山，色美形胜，山石嶙峋清奇，绵延的山势如同巨幅幔帐，连同它东西南三面的小山，合围起一片河水丰沛的广袤腹地。在古人的风水观念中，山是气之源，环山抱水则藏风聚气，好风水求的就是气。气在天，化为日月星辰；气在地，形成山川河流、花草走兽。这里便是适配帝王的上佳风水宝地。

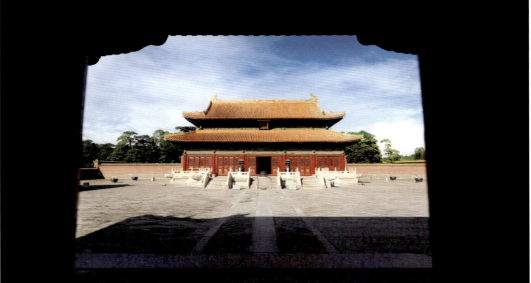

Taining Mountain was later renamed as Yongning Mountain. It is spectacular in colors and shapes, almost like a giant painting. Along with the three hills on the east, south and west, it creates beautiful hinterland with lakes enclosed. In the concept of ancient Fengshui, the mountain is the source of qi (air). Surrounded by the mountains and holding the water is to good Fengshui to gather qi. When qi is up in the sky, it becomes the sun, moon and stars, and when qi is down on the ground, it forms mountains, rivers, flowers, plants and animals. This is the perfect auspicious land for emperors.

　　从现代科学来看，清西陵和清东陵一样，确实是一片水土优厚的土地。现代气象资料显示，东陵所在的遵化曾经是燕山山脉中降水量最充足、植被最好的一段。西陵所在的易县同样也曾是太行山中降水丰沛、土壤肥沃的一段。

From the perspective of modern science, the Western Royal Tombs and the Eastern Royal Tombs of the Qing Dynasty are both indeed lands with abundant water and fertile soil. Meteorological data analysis shows that Zunhua, where the Eastern Royal Tombs were located, was once the section with the most abundant rainfall and the best plant coverage among the Yanshan Mountain Area. Yixian County, where the Western Royal Tombs were located, also had the most abundant rainfall and the most fertile soil among the Taihang Mountain Area.

　　这两处群山环绕，西面、北面的山高大巍峨，南面、东面的山矮小峻秀，形成了前方略显开敞的半封闭式围合结构。这种地势既可以阻挡西北的风沙寒流，又能充分地迎纳东南而来的阳光和雨水，且周围多有大河萦绕，重重汇聚，婉转有情。气候宜人，水草丰沛，是一个理想的生存和居住环境。

　　These two places are surrounded by mountains. The mountains in the west and north are high and majestic, while the mountains in the south and east are low but beautiful. This landscape has formed a semi-enclosed layout to protect the mausoleums. This type of terrain structure can not only block the wind, sand and cold current from the northwest, but also fully welcome the sunshine and rain from the southeast. With the pleasant climate and abundant plants, it is an ideal environment for living.

1730年，雍正帝的泰陵兴工营建，历时八载方才完工。泰陵的中轴线好似一条纽带，串联起七十多座建筑，是西陵中规模最宏大、形制最完备的第一陵。

In 1730, the construction of the Tailing Tomb for Emperor Yongzheng started and it took eight years to complete. The central axis of the Tailing Tomb is like a linking belt, connecting more than 70 buildings. It is the largest and most well-appointed Number One tomb in the Western Royal Tombs of the Qing Dynasty.

在后世人看来，雍正帝具有极高的艺术修养与品位。他的泰陵自然建得既合规制，又别有意趣。

In the eyes of later generations, Emperor Yongzheng had a very high artistic accomplishment and taste. His Tailing Tomb was therefore built within regulations, but also interesting and innovating.

火焰牌坊是泰陵的起点，也是整个西陵的起点。这座青白石牌坊的额枋上装饰着三只火焰宝珠，上面雕刻着火焰纹饰，据说象征逢凶化吉。这是泰陵不同于其他皇陵的独特建置，暗含着对江山社稷的美好期许。

The flame archway was the starting point of the Tailing Tomb and also the starting point of the entire Western Royal Tombs. The headings of the grey-white stone archway were decorated with three flame orbs, which were engraved with flame patterns and were said to symbolize good luck. This is a unique construction that makes Tailing Tomb stand out from other imperial mausoleums and it implied a good expectation for the ruling of the Qing Dynasty.

五孔拱桥后，坐落着三架仿木结构牌坊，与大红门一起形成了一个四合院落。这种形式的石牌坊目前在国内仅存这一处。穿大碑楼、过七孔石拱桥，邂逅五对石像生，这是乾隆十三年乾隆帝为父亲补立的。经龙凤门，到神道碑亭，这组建筑群可以说是泰陵的先导空间。

Behind the five-aperture arch bridge are three faux wooden arches which together with the big red gate form a quadrangle courtyard. This form of stone archway is the only currently existing one in China. After passing through the Dabei building and crossing the seven-aperture stone arch bridge, one can reach five pairs of stone statues which were built by Emperor Qianlong to remember his father. From the Dragon and Phoenix Gate to the Divine Road Stele Pavilion, this group of buildings are the personalized pilot space of the Tailing Tomb.

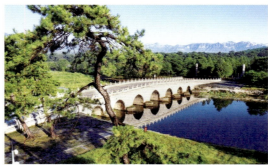

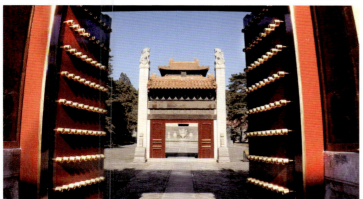

从神道碑亭往北至宝顶，是泰陵的主体区域宫殿区。在先导空间，皇帝可以任性，用一些改动来彰显自己的喜好与性格。到了宫殿区，就只有陵寝规制带来的模式化的一致性。

From the Divine Road Stele Pavilion to the royal crown roof in the north is the palace area and the main area of the Tailing Tomb. In the pilot space, the emperor could do as he wished and use some unique designs to show his preferences and personality. However, in the palace area, emperors had to follow the regulations of mausoleums to maintain consistency.

　　神道碑亭往北沿中轴线，自大月台过隆恩门，穿东西焚帛炉、东西配殿，方至隆恩殿。再经琉璃花门、二柱门，祭台、方城、明楼才能抵达终点宝城宝顶。虽然这是清帝陵寝的标准配置，但泰陵仍然得到建筑学家刘敦桢的好评，"规模最为宏阔，规制更为整齐"，堪称清代诸帝陵的"典范"。"典范"，能作为典型范例，泰陵兼具美观与规整，体现典雅与宏伟，有着大而庄重的气质与小却精致的意趣。

　　Moving north along the central axis from the Divine Road Stele Pavilion, one can pass through the Dayue platform, the Long'en Gate, the pair of tribute furnaces, the pair of side halls, then reach the Long'en Palace. After passing through the glazed flower gate, the double column gate, the altar, the square city and the Minglou Building, one can reach the top of the sacred building which is the end point of the mausoleum. Although this is the standard configuration of the mausoleums for emperors in the Qing Dynasty, the Tailing Tomb was still highly praised by Liu Dunzhen, an architect, "Its scale is the biggest and its layout is well organized." It is the representative mausoleum for emperors in the Qing Dynasty. As the model mausoleum, the Tailing Tomb is both beautiful and regular, reflecting grandeur with a large and solemn temperament while showing elegance with exquisite characters.

为雍正帝寻找吉壤的是他的十三弟怡亲王允祥，怡亲王曾辅佐雍正帝承袭大统，后又辅政八年，日夜操劳，鞠躬尽瘁。泰陵选址确定后，雍正帝在泰陵附近选了一块"中吉之地"赐予怡亲王，他坚辞不受。最后，他的园寝建在了西陵30千米外的涞水县娄村满族乡。怡亲王园寝占地600多亩，有30多座建筑，是清代规模最大的宗室园寝，超过清代亲王园寝规制数倍。逾越规制的背后是一段兄弟情深，雍正帝用死后的殊荣表达了对这个弟弟的爱护。

It was Emperor Yongzheng's thirteenth younger brother, Prince Yi named Yunxiang, who found this auspicious land for the emperor. Prince Yi once assisted Emperor Yongzheng in inheriting the imperial power, and later assisted Yongzheng for eight years with loyalty and full support. After the location of the Tailing Tomb was determined, Emperor Yongzheng chose a land of blessing near the Tailing Tomb and gifted it to Prince Yi, but Prince Yi declined it. In the end, Price Yi's mausoleum was built in Loucun Manchu Township in Laishui County, 30 kilometers away from the Western Royal Tombs. Covering an area of more than 600 mu, with more than 30 buildings, Prince Yi's mausoleum was the largest royal family tomb besides an emperor's imperial tomb in the Qing Dynasty, exceeding the regulations of the Qing Dynasty as prince tomb for several times. This exceptional tomb scale shows the close brotherhood between Emperor Yongzheng and Prince Yi. Emperor Yongzheng expressed his love for this younger brother by honoring him in the afterlife.

按照乾隆帝定下的"昭穆葬"之制，乾隆帝归葬东陵，他的儿子嘉庆帝归于西陵，即昌陵。

According to the "Zhaomu" burial system set by himself, Emperor Qianlong was buried in the Eastern Royal Tombs, and his son Emperor Jiaqing was buried in the Changling Tomb in the Western Royal Tombs.

在故宫收藏的宝藏中，有一项世界记忆遗产《样式雷图档》，其中便有昌陵地宫四门九券的设计图纸。"样式雷"是清朝最杰出的建筑设计品牌，嘉庆帝的昌陵是他们的第一个陵寝杰作，由第四代传人雷家玺主持设计建造。手稿中的"现场活计图"，也就是常说的施工现场进展图，展示了帝陵从选地、基础开挖、修建地宫到屋面完成的全过程。

Among the ancient treasures collected in the Forbidden City, there is a World Memory Heritage *Style Lei Blueprints* which includes the floor plans and design sketches of the four gates and nine Quans of the Changling Underground Palace. Style Lei is the most outstanding architectural design brand in the Qing Dynasty. Emperor Jiaqing's Changling Tomb was their first masterpiece of mausoleum, which was designed and constructed by Lei Jiaxi, the fourth-generation descendant of the Lei family. The "construction site work notes" recorded the entire process of the imperial construction from site selection, foundation excavation, construction of the underground palace to the completion of the roof.

之前，人们误认为中国古代建筑完全依靠工匠的经验修建而成。"样式雷"的图档证明了中国古代建筑不仅有精密的设计，其中还蕴藏了大智慧。

In the past, people mistakenly thought that ancient Chinese buildings were built entirely based on the experience of craftsmen. Style Lei's records proved that ancient Chinese architecture not only had sophisticated design, but also contained great wisdom and planning.

　　昌陵地宫结构宏大、四门九券雕刻精细。陵寝券顶是用一块块砖砌筑的，合拢这样的券顶是相当困难的，但雷家玺成功将金券合拢，堪称奇迹。

The underground palace of Changling Tomb has a grand structure with exquisitely carved four gates and nine Quans. Quan, the arched top of the building, was built with bricks, making it quite difficult to close such a roof. Lei Jiaxi succeeded in closing the golden Quan, making it a miracle in architectural history.

　　昌菱隆恩殿的地面也是"样式雷"别出心裁的设计。西陵其余帝陵的隆恩殿皆为金砖铺地，昌陵则用产自河南的豆瓣石砌铺，石面黄色，缀以天然紫色花纹，有"满堂宝石"之美誉。

The floor of the Long'en Palace in Changling Tomb was also ingeniously designed. The Long'en Palaces of other imperial mausoleums in the Western Royal Tombs were paved with gold bricks, while the one in Changling Tomb was paved with bean stones from Henan Province. The surface of this jewelry-like stone was yellow and decorated with natural purple patterns.

昌西陵的回音壁的回音效果极佳，为清代陵寝中的特例。

The echoing effect of the Echo Wall in the Changxiling Tomb was excellent, which made it exceptional among all the mausoleums in the Qing Dynasty.

　　道光帝的慕陵由"样式雷"第五代传人雷景修主持设计建造，是清代帝陵中风格最为独特的一座，处处有着违背皇陵规制的设计和看似低调实则奢华的材料。

　　Emperor Daoguang's Muling Tomb was designed and built by Lei Jingxiu, the fifth-generation descendant of Style Lei. It is the most unique style among the imperial mausoleums in the Qing Dynasty. It was hidden with personalized designs and luxury materials.

　　慕陵坐落在一大片苍翠的松林中，整体来看，建筑规模不大，紧凑精巧，其实里面的单体建筑却大有乾坤，许多建筑都拥有打破常规的形制与建筑细节。

　　The Muling Tomb is located among a large field of verdant pine trees. Seen from the outside, the building is small in scale, compact and delicate. In fact, each building inside is hidden with innovative designs and details breaking traditional mausoleum regulations.

道光帝亲自参与了慕陵的建筑规制和装饰设计。据清宫档案《上谕档》记载，他下了一道圣谕："酌改宝城规制。方城、明楼、穿堂诸券、琉璃花门、石像生俱著撤去。"裁撤之后，慕陵的建筑只剩下27座，不到泰陵的一半。帝陵的宝顶前，通常有方城明楼，这是整个陵区最高的建筑物，里面树立着刻有皇帝庙号的朱砂牌，可以说是陵寝的门面。

　　Emperor Daoguang personally participated in the architectural and decoration design of the Muling Tomb. According to the Qing Palace archives *Shangyu Records*, he issued an imperial announcement: "Amendments are made and the square city, the Minglou Building, the Hall of Quans, the glazed flower gate, and the stone statues are to be removed." After the amendments, there were only 27 buildings left in the Muling Tomb, less than half of those in the Tailing Tomb. In front of the Sacred Building, there was usually a Square City Minglou Building, which was the tallest building in the entire mausoleum. With a cinnabar tablet engraved with the emperor's posthumous title, here is also the facade of the mausoleum.

慕陵地宫只建有方形大月台和圆台形宝顶一座，尺度也仅有其他帝陵的一半，这是清朝帝陵中的孤例。

The Muling Tomb's Underground Palace only has a square platform and a round-roof sacred building with a scale half of those in other imperial mausoleums, which is a unique case.

陵寝的隆恩殿，由重檐改为单檐，与其他帝陵相比，外表简陋。可实际上，这座隆恩殿恰恰是清朝所有帝陵中最壮丽奢华的一座。整座大殿及其东西配殿，全部用金丝楠木建造而成。

The Long'en Palace of the mausoleum was changed from double eaves to single eaves. Compared with other imperial mausoleums, its appearance was rather simple. But in fact, this Long'en Palace was precisely the most magnificent and luxurious one of all the imperial mausoleums in the Qing Dynasty. The entire palace and its pair of side halls were all made of Phoebe Zhennan wood.

清西陵

金丝楠木，产于四川、广西、云南、贵州等地的深山，木纹中排列着结晶体，在阳光照耀下宛若金丝浮现，有雍容华贵之感。因其生长慢、产量少、运输难，早在明代就已经是稀有植物。据粗略估计，慕陵隆恩殿共使用金丝楠木约1500立方米。

The Phoebe Zhennan wood was collected in the deep mountains from places such as Sichuan, Guangxi, Yunnan and Guizhou. Crystals were mixed in the wood grain, making it glow like golden threads in the sunlight, giving it a sense of grace and luxury. Due to its long growing period, low yield and the difficulty of transportation, it had been a rare plant since the Ming Dynasty. According to a rough estimate, about 1,500 cubic meters of golden silk Phoebe Zhennan were used in the Muling Tomb's Long'en Palace.

慕陵隆恩殿的雕刻也极尽奢华。八百余块天花板布满了精致的木雕龙，龙头凸出平面，极具立体感。门窗隔扇和雀替上也雕满了龙，整个隆恩殿共有木龙1316条，形状、姿态各不相同。据说，道光帝此前在东陵修宝华峪地宫时曾出现渗水事故，于是他大量雕龙，让群龙在天上争水，以解决慕陵地宫的水患。

The carvings inside the Long'en Palace were also extremely luxurious. More than 800 pieces of ceiling were covered with exquisite woodcarving dragons, and the dragon heads protruded from the plane, which was stereoscopic and vivid. There were also dragons carved on the doors, windows, partitions and frames. There were 1,316 wooden dragons in the entire Long'en Palace, with different shapes and postures. It is said that Emperor Daoguang had a water seepage accident when he was repairing the Baohua Valley Underground Palace in the Eastern Royal Tombs, therefore he requested to carve a large number of dragons and let the dragons compete for water in the sky to solve the flooding of the underground palace in Muling Tomb.

低调奢华的慕陵，就连看似普通的围墙也暗藏玄机。不同于皇陵围墙的朱红，慕陵的围墙呈淡灰色。通常的围墙一层砖一层灰，表面非常粗糙，需要抹上红色涂料加以遮盖。

The low-key but luxurious Muling Tomb had hidden secrets even in the seemingly ordinary walls. Unlike the vermilion walls in other imperial mausoleums, the walls in Muling Tomb were pale gray. Usually there was one layer of brick and one layer of ash alternately on the wall and they were finally covered with red paint to smoothen the surface.

慕陵的围墙则用的是最高级、最讲究的一种工艺——干摆墙。将砖块打磨到一边厚一边薄，再一层层垒上去，用灰浆填满中间出现的凹槽。这种围墙费工费时，造价之高昂远超其他帝陵。

However, the walls of Muling Tomb were built with the most advanced and exquisite craftsmanship at that time—dry swing wall. The bricks were ground so that one end was thick and the other end was thin, then they were used to build up the wall layer by layer, filling the grooves that appeared within the mortar. This kind of wall was extremely time-consuming, and cost much higher than ordinary walls in other imperial mausoleums.

道光帝的陵寝，经历两次修建，原材料贵重，工艺高超，造价高达240万两白银，比乾隆帝以华丽著称的裕陵还多了37万两。

Emperor Daoguang's mausoleum was renovated twice. With the luxury raw materials and superb craftsmanship, the construction cost as high as 2.4 million taels of silver, which was 370,000 taels more than the famous Yuling Tomb of Emperor Qianlong.

光绪帝的崇陵是中国帝陵营建史上浓重而苍凉的尾音，印上了新旧交替的时代烙印。

Emperor Guangxu's Chongling Tomb was a heavy and desolate ending in the history of the construction of Chinese imperial mausoleums, marking the shifting point from an old era to a new one.

崇陵所在地金龙峪，曾多次被列入备选吉地，但每次都会落选，这说明金龙峪不是一处上吉之壤。可这里最终成了光绪帝的吉地。崇陵修建期间恰逢1911年，清帝被迫退位，工程也不得已中断一年。

Jinlong Valley, where Chongling Tomb was located, had been listed as a backup location for mausoleums for many times by previous emperors, but was never picked before, which suggested that Jinlong Valley was not a perfect choice for auspicious land. However, it was eventually used as the auspicious land for Emperor Guangxu's tomb. The construction of the Chongling Tomb coincided with 1911, in which year the emperor of the Qing Dynasty was forced to abdicate, and the project had to be ceased for a year.

　　崇陵模仿同治帝的惠陵而建，少了大碑亭、石像生等建筑。崇陵的隆恩殿木料均为异常珍贵的铜藻、铁藻，俗有"铜梁铁柱"之称。

　　The Chongling Tomb was built in imitation of the Emperor Tongzhi's Huiling Tomb, without the monumental pavilion, stone statues and some other buildings. The wood material of the Long'en Palace in Chongling Tomb was very precious copper algae and iron algae, which made the palace structure commonly known as "copper beams and iron pillars."

　　历史的新变化也赋予崇陵一些独到之处，民国的设计理念与技术手段在崇陵多有体现。崇陵有比较完备的排水系统。所有宫殿的基座，都用青砖砌成2米宽的散水，以便快速排走积聚的雨水。地宫凿出14个排水口，联通明楼前的龙须沟，随时可将地宫可能存在的渗水排出。隆恩殿的墙上，也建有铜钱形通风口，以便保持殿内木料的干燥。

　　The changes brought by the new era also endowed the Chongling Tomb with some unique features. The design concepts and construction techniques from the period of the Republic of China were reflected in the Chongling Tomb. The Chongling Tomb had a relatively complete drainage system. The bases of all palaces were built with black bricks to form a 2-meter-wide drainage path to quickly drain the accumulated rainwater. The underground palace had 14 drainage outlets, which were connected to the Longxu ditch in front of the Minglou Building to drain out potential seepage in the underground palace. There were also copper coin-shaped vents on the walls of the Long'en Palace to keep wooden constructions inside dry.

西陵的建筑多为土木结构，木料用量极大，通风极为重要。

Most civil structures in the Western Royal Tombs used large amount of wood, therefore ventilation was extremely important.

墙上的透风，就专为通风而建。透风其实是一块带有镂空雕刻的砖。早前的能工巧匠，巧妙地控制着每栋建筑中木柱与墙体的距离，尽量维持在5厘米左右，同时在柱底位置对应的墙体位置留一个砖洞口，尺寸约为15厘米宽，20厘米高。为了外表美观，工匠们多采用刻有纹饰的镂空砖雕来砌筑这个洞口，这个带有图纹的砖就被称为透风。俗语"世上没有不透风的墙"讲的便是这个现象。

The ventilation on the wall was designed for this purpose. The vents were actually bricks with hollow carvings. The skilled craftsmen carefully calculated the distance between the wooden column and the wall in each building, trying to maintain it around 5 centimeters, and at the same time leaving a brick hole sized at 15 centimeters wide and 20 centimeters high at the position of the wall corresponding to the bottom of the column. In order to guarantee a beautiful appearance, craftsmen used hollow brick carvings with patterns to create the hole. These patterned bricks serve as the ventilation system and allow wind to pass the wall. The Chinese saying "wind always sneaks through walls" speaks of this phenomenon.

崇陵有一份只属于自己的殊荣，一片白皮松林。这些珍贵的树木代表着一份难得的师生情。恰逢时变，崇陵的规划中并没有列入植树这一项，光绪的老师梁鼎芬几经努力，筹来善款，亲自栽种了白皮松林和四万余株翠柏。只是随着清王朝的消亡，西陵树木的管理日渐松懈，终不能保全银松翠柏的郁茂。

The Chongling Tomb had certain characters that other mausoleums didn't have—the white bark pine forest. These precious trees represented a historic teacher-student friendship. Because of the troubled historical background, the construction plan for Chongling Tomb did not include planting work. Liang Dingfen, the teacher of Emperor Guangxu, raised money and planted a white bark pine forest and more than 40,000 cypress trees. However, with the demise of the Qing Dynasty, the planting management in the Western Royal Tombs became chaotic, and those silver pines and cypresses could not be well preserved in the end.

梁鼎芬郁郁而终后，葬在崇陵右旁的山上，永远地陪伴着自己的学生。

After Liang Dingfen passed away gloomily, he was buried on the mountain on the right next to the Chongling Tomb and accompanied his student forever.

"陵寝以风水为重，荫护以树木为先"，清廷把树木看作西陵不可或缺的元素之一。在泰陵修建之时就广植松树，每年还拨专款用于维护。

"The Fengshui determines the mausoleum and plants add more to Fengshui." The Qing Dynasty regarded trees as one of the indispensable elements of the Western Royal Tombs. Therefore, when the Tailing Tomb was built, pine trees were widely planted, and special funds were allocated every year for maintenance.

今天，西陵密布着15000余株平均年龄在三百岁左右的古松，20余万株幼松。古松中名气最大的当数泰陵宝城旁的"卧龙松"。它蹬墙基，倚城墙，酷似卧龙。松林随山起伏，顺道蜿蜒，烘云托月，成为西陵一道独特的风景。斗转星移，岁月更迭，古松始终陪伴着这座典雅凝重、气势恢宏的庞大建筑群，注视着一个王朝离去的背影。

Today, there are more than 15,000 ancient pine trees with an average age of about 300 years old and more than 200,000 young pine trees in the Western Royal Tombs. The most famous one among the ancient pine trees is the "Wolong" pine next to Tailing Tomb's Treasure Chamber. It grows along the wall base and leans against the wall, just like a sitting dragon. The pine forest undulates up and down with the mountains, winding along the road, as if reaching out to the clouds and moon, making it a unique scenery of the Western Royal Tombs. Time goes by and those pine trees have always accompanied this elegant and magnificent mausoleum, witnessing the demise of the Qing Dynasty.

　　守护陵寝的还有守陵人。无论是东陵还是西陵，建设伊始，保卫、管理皇陵的人员便源源不断地到来。他们在东陵、西陵附近定居，形成村落，与皇陵相伴相生，衍生出自己独特的生活习惯与文化。

There were also mausoleum keepers. Whether it was in the Eastern Royal Tombs or the Western Royal Tombs, at the beginning of the construction, people who defended and managed the imperial tombs came continuously. They settled down in the vicinity of the tombs and formed villages. They lived along with the imperial tombs and derived their own unique living habits and culture.

　　忠义村、凤凰台等十几个大大小小的满族村落呈环绕之势，护卫着西陵。这里居住的大多是当年守陵人的后代。1730年，清廷修建泰陵时，在梁各庄设立专门的保护机构——泰宁协，逐渐把这里原来的十九个自然村庄迁出禁区之外，改由西陵的守卫管理人员入驻。

More than a dozen Manchu villages such as Zhongyi Village and Fenghuangtai Village were established around to guard the Western Royal Tombs. Most of the people living here are the descendants of the mausoleum keepers. In 1730, when the Tailing Tomb was built, the rulers established a special protection agency—the Taining Managing Office in Lianggezhuang, and gradually drove out the former residents in the original nineteen natural villages and replaced them with guards and managers for the Western Royal Tombs.

1737年，泰陵建成，设立专门的管理机构护卫陵寝。每一座陵寝还会设立内务府、礼部和八旗三座分支保卫管理机构。为此，清廷将东北、北京等地的八旗人员调拨到西陵各保护管理机构中任职，从事陵寝的祭祀、保卫、维修等工作，形成了一整套庞大健全的守陵队伍。这些陵寝保卫管理机构，就是今天清西陵守陵村落的前身。

In 1737, the construction of Tailing Tomb was completed and a special management agency was established to guard the tombs. Each mausoleum inside also set up three branches of the Ministry of Internal Affairs, the Ministry of Rites and the Eight Banners. To this end, the rulers redeployed people of the Eight Banners from Northeast China, Beijing and other places to work in various protection and management institutions of the Western Royal Tombs, to supervise on sacrifice, protection, maintenance and other work of the mausoleum. This large and sound tomb guarding team was the predecessor of today's guardian villages.

前些年，清西陵开始了一场中华人民共和国成立以来最大规模的修缮。经历至少上百年的自然老化之后，清西陵建筑上的地仗出现了空鼓、剥离、脱落，以致其上的油饰和彩画出现诸多病害，需要专业的人员进行保护性修复。从事这项修复工作的匠人大多都是当时守陵人的后代，在做修复工作之前，他们早已耳濡目染，那些关于修复的流程与讲究已烂熟于心，所有的操作工序也经过无数次的演练与试验。

A few years ago, the largest renovation work since the founding of the People's Republic of China began in the Western Royal Tombs. After at least a hundred years of natural aging, the ground base on the buildings in

the mausoleums have been hollowed out, peeled off and fallen off, resulting in many erosion on the oil ornaments and colored paintings above, which required professional personnel to restore. Most of the craftsmen engaged in this restoration work were descendants of the mausoleum keepers at that time. Before doing the restoration work, they were already familiar with the process and cautions, and had practiced many times before.

描画、打底、上色，一笔一笔的勾勒中，时间缓慢流过。那些古老的技艺，似乎从来未曾走远，一代又一代的传承与演练，只为等待这一刻的重逢。

Drawing, priming and coloring—each stroke reminds people of the craftsmanship in the past. Those ancient skills seem to have never gone far, and they have been passed down and practiced from generation to generation just to wait for this moment of reunion.

"蒸羊羔，蒸熊掌，蒸鹿尾儿，烧花鸭，烧雏鸡，烧子鹅，卤煮咸鸭，酱鸡，腊肉，松花小肚儿……""蒸鹿尾儿"这个经常在相声里出现的菜肴，冬至这一天出现在了凤凰台村的宴席上。

"Steamed lamb, steamed bear paw, steamed deer tail, roasted duck, roasted chicken, roasted goose, stewed salted duck, salted chicken, bacon, flavored pork belly..." "Steamed deer tail" is often the dish that appears in the Chinese cross talk now appeared at the banquet in Fenghuangtai Village on the day of winter solstice.

凤凰台村的村民都是守陵人的后代，他们把满族饮食文化和习俗带到了这里。两百年过去了，满族民俗与风味美食也被一一继承了下来，与现代营养学相结合，逐渐形成了品种多样、讲究礼仪的饮食风格。今天，"蒸鹿尾儿"等原汁原味的满族特色菜已经成为凤凰台村的民俗名片。

The villagers of Fenghuangtai Village are all descendants of the mausoleum keepers. Two hundred years have passed. Manchu folk customs and delicacies have been inherited one after another. Combined with modern nutrition, a variety of food styles and etiquette have been gradually formed. Today, authentic Manchu specialties such as "steamed deer tail" have become the folk signature of the Fenghuangtai Village.

不远处的忠义村，他们的拿手绝活儿是一项古老演出，国家级非物质文化遗产——摆字龙灯。

In Zhongyi Village not far away, their specialty is an ancient performance and a national intangible cultural heritage—"Baizi Longdeng"—a word spelling with dragon lantern dance.

据说，乾隆年间为纪念雍正帝在位十三年的文治武功，将一条完整的龙断为十三节，每节用细绳和三个竹环相连，外加领龙绣球一个，因此又称为"十三节龙"。龙的每一节可以作为汉字一个笔画，绣球为笔画"点"，在舞动中可摆出各种十三画以内的汉字。

It is said that during Qianlong's reign, in order to commemorate Emperor Yongzheng's accomplishment in the thirteen years of his governance, a complete dragon was broken into thirteen sections. Each section was connected by three bamboo rings and a string, then a hydrangea was added to lead the dragon. Therefore, it is also known as "Thirteen-section Dragons." Each section of the dragon can be used as a stroke of a Chinese character, and the hydrangea is the stroke's leading point. During the dance, various Chinese characters within thirteen strokes can be displayed.

每年，清东陵景区都会举行一场祭祀表演，西陵东韩村的非遗艺人都会受邀前去表演，这也是清东陵与清西陵两地之间的一种特有的交流方式。

Every year, a sacrificial performance is held in the scenic area of the Eastern Royal Tombs. The intangible cultural heritage artists from Donghan Village of the Western Royal Tombs are invited to perform there. This is a special way of communication between the two locations.

东韩村传承的这项国家级非物质文化遗产名叫拾幡古乐。拾幡古乐本是清朝皇家礼仪音乐，由皇宫流入民间，从建立之初传承至今历经九代。拾幡古乐的舞曲保存至今的只有十余首，曲调哀而不伤，婉转悠扬，又称"神仙曲"。

The national intangible cultural heritage inherited by Donghan Village is called Shifan Ancient Music. Shifan Ancient Music was originally the royal ceremonial music of the Qing Dynasty. It spread from the palace to the common people and it has been passed down for nine generations since its establishment. There are only more than ten dance songs of Shifan Ancient Music that have been preserved so far. The tone of the music is blue but not sad, which is also known as the "music of immortals."

在清东陵，当年守陵人的后裔大多居住在遵化东陵满族乡、马兰峪镇等地。马兰峪镇当时是东陵承办事务衙门和孝陵礼部营房、孝东陵内务府营房所在地，清代皇家宫廷特色的纯手工金银器加工技艺在这里得到了延续与传承。皇家金银细工，采用手工錾刻工艺，是皇家造办处独有的秘制工艺之一，成品做工精湛，纹饰精美，造型典雅，极富寓意，同样是我国非物质文化遗产。

In the Eastern Royal Tombs of the Qing Dynasty, most of the descendants of the mausoleum keepers lived in Manchu Township and Malan Valley Town in Zunhua. At that time, Malan Valley Town was the location of the administration office and the barracks of the Ministry of Rites of the Xiaoling Tomb, and the barracks of the Household Office of the Xiaodongling Tomb in the Eastern Royal Tombs. The pure hand-made gold and silverware processing skills of the royal family from the Qing Dynasty were inherited and passed on here. Royal gold and silver were exquisite and required highly skillful craftsmanship in hand engraving, which made royal engraving the unique secret craftsmanship of the Royal Manufacture Office. The finished works are exquisitely beautiful and well made in colors and shapes, making it also a national intangible cultural heritage in China.

金银器制匠人用手的温度与心的深情为金银赋予灵魂，在光阴中一笔一画地将美丽与韵致錾刻在金银器作品上；彩画工匠用虔诚与匠心延续着古老建筑的生命；而那些古乐、古曲也带着最初的期许，始终萦绕在这片静默的土地周围。

Gold and silver are endowed with soul through craftsmen's hands and hearts, and are engraved with beauty and charm through time. Color painting craftsmen commemorate the ancient peers by restoring the ancient buildings with piety and ingenuity. And those ancient music and songs also carry their original expectation, and continue the beautiful story on this peaceful land.

时光远去，小树成了古木，陵寝成了园林，唯有建筑，唯有艺术，穿越时空，带着历史的回音，讲述着古老的情愫，打动着天地与人心。

Time goes by. Small trees have become ancient trees; mausoleums have become gardens; only architecture and art have traveled through time with echoes of history, telling ancient stories to the world, touching the world and the hearts.

6

North of the Great River: World Cultural Heritage
The Grand Canal

大运河

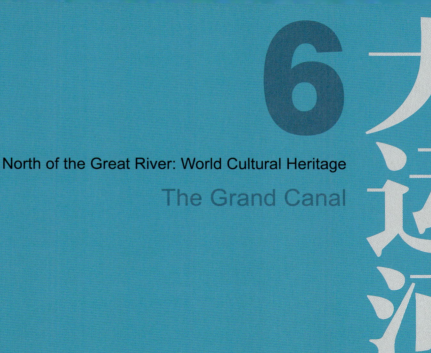

这是一首永不止歇的大地史诗，从公元前五世纪开始书写，一脉活水襟江南、越中原、带燕赵，催生出一座座文化名城，承载着无数繁华的盛景，沉淀了无数兴衰的记忆。

作为世界上建造时间最早、使用最久、空间跨度最大的人工运河，除了人们熟知的京杭大运河，中国大运河还包括隋唐运河、浙东运河在内的广阔空间。今天，这条大河与它所生发的文明仍然生机勃勃，一如既往地滋养着生活在两岸的三亿多中国人。

这个伟大工程有六分之一经过河北，包括隋唐大运河和京杭大运河两部分。曾经，沿着运河，河北人打开了视野，北上南下，走向世界。

这是地球上对自然地理面貌改变最大的人类工程，它在主要大江大河皆东流的神州大地上以连接南北的姿态跨越地球10多个纬度，连通海河、黄河、淮河、长江、钱塘江五大自然水系。中国人将智慧、勇气、决心倾注在3200千米的河道中，与大自然共同刻画出这一奇观。

This is the project done by man that has brought the biggest natural and geographical change on Earth. While most rivers in China flow from west towards east, this canal spans more than 10 latitudes and connects five major natural river systems including Haihe River, the Yellow River, Huaihe River, Yangtze River and Qiantang River. The Chinese people infused their wisdom, courage and determination into this 3,200-kilometer river course to create this spectacle together with nature.

这是一首永不止歇的大地史诗，从公元前五世纪开始书写，一脉活水襟江南、越中原、苕燕赵，催生出一座座文化名城，承载着无数繁华的盛景，沉淀了无数兴衰的记忆。

The canal is a never-ending epic of the Earth, written since the fifth century BC. The continuous flow of water cultivated Jiangnan (regions south of the Yangtse River), the Central Plains and Yanzhao (present Hebei), giving birth to numerous famous cultural cities, accompanying countless prosperous views, and witnessing countless memories of history.

作为世界上建造时间最早、使用最久、空间跨度最大的人工运河，除了人们熟知的京杭大运河，中国大运河还包括隋唐运河、浙东运河在内的广阔空间。今天，这条大河与它所生发的文明仍然生机勃勃，一如既往地滋养着生活在两岸的三亿多中国人。

As the oldest artificial canal in the world, the longest in use and the largest in space, besides the well-known Jinghang (Beijing-Hangzhou) Canal, the Chinese Grand Canal also includes the Suitang (of the Sui and Tang Dynasties) Canals and the Zhedong (eastern Zhejiang) Canal. Today, the Grand Canal and the civilization it spawned are still full of vitality, nourishing more than 300 million Chinese people along the canal.

这个伟大工程有六分之一经过河北，包括隋唐大运河和京杭大运河两部分。曾经，沿着运河，河北人打开了视野，北上南下，走向世界。

One-sixth of the Grand Canal passes through Hebei, including the Suitang Canals and the Jinghang Canal. Once upon a time, along the canal, people of Hebei traveled around the nation and widened their horizon.

2021年夏末，在廊坊市香河县北运河香河中心码头，一艘画舫悠悠入水，在中断五十多年之后的这个夏天，大运河北运河段恢复了通航功能。

By the end of the summer in 2021, at the central pier of the North Canal in Xianghe County of Langfang City, a painted boat entered the water, marking the reuse of the canal after stopping navigation for more than 50 years.

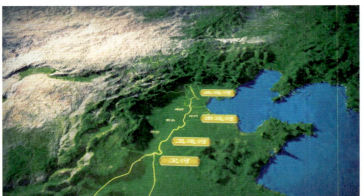

沿河北上，不远处就是杨洼闸，这个15孔的拦河建筑物是北运河京冀分界点，也是大运河河北段的最北端。大运河在河北境内分为北运河、南运河、卫运河、卫河四大河段，流经廊坊、仓州、衡水、邢台、邯郸五市，行水530多千米。

Going up the canal northward, one can see the Yangwa Gate. This 15-hole river barrage is the dividing point between Beijing and Hebei on the North Canal, which is also the northernmost point of the Hebei section of the Grand Canal. The Hebei section of the Grand Canal is divided into four river sections, namely, the North Canal, the South Canal, the Wei Canal and the Wei River. Its river course stretches to more than 530 kilometers and passes through five cities including Langfang, Cangzhou, Hengshui, Xingtai and Handan.

　　静水流深，大运河一如千年之前，画舫游走，涟漪一圈一圈地荡漾开来，这是大运河特有的年轮。

Still waters run deep. The Grand Canal still functions as it once did a thousand years ago. The painted boats shuttled. The ripples are the unique growth ring of the Grand Canal.

　　从公元204年开始，曹操建邺都，筑三台，从此邺城成为中国北方的政治经济文化中心，不仅留下了建安文学的辉煌，也为中国北方运河的大规模开凿书写了肇始的篇章。为了北驱乌桓，一统天下，曹操先后开凿白沟、利漕渠、平虏渠、泉州渠和新河五条人工漕运河渠，把华北大平原上的滹沱河、漳水、古易水、潞水等水系互相贯通，成为他统一北方的漕运利器。

Ever since Cao Cao built Ye as a second capital and Three Terraces in 204AD, Ye became the political, economic and cultural center of northern China, initiating the splendorous Jian'an literature period and writing the first chapter for the construction of the Canal in northern China. In order to drive out the Wuhuan Nomads in the north and unify the nation, Cao Cao dug five artificial canals, namely, Baigou, Licao, Pinglu, Quanzhou and Xinhe. These canals connected the water systems on the North China Plain, such as Hutuo River, Zhangshui River, Yishui River and Lu River, providing a powerful military tool of canal transportation for Cao Cao to unify the north.

历史远去，光阴湮没了军功，岁月斑驳了城池。这些人工开挖的河道，在以后的日子里一次次地被唤醒重生，冠以不同的名称，成为国家新的动脉。

Time goes by. History has put military achievements into oblivion. Years have mottled ancient towns. These artificial rivers have been awakened and reborn again and again throughout history and have been given different names. They have become new arteries of the nation.

公元605年，隋炀帝杨广开挖隋唐大运河。这条河以洛阳为中心，一撇一捺如同"人"字，一撇向南，尽头是今天的杭州。一捺是永济渠，经过河北直到今天的北京。

In 605, Yang Guang, Emperor of the Sui Dynasty started the construction of the Suitang Canal. The construction started in Luoyang. The canal stretched in the shape of the Chinese character "人", one course stretching south to the present Hangzhou, the other stretching northwards up the Yongji River to Beijing through Hebei.

公元1272年，元世祖忽必烈定都大都，也就是今天的北京。自此，这座城市正式成为影响后世近千年的国家政治中心。

In 1272, Kublai Khan, Yuanshizu of the Yuan Dynasty, established its capital in Dadu, which is today's Beijing. Since then, this city has officially become a national political center that has influenced later generations for nearly a thousand years.

此时，承担着都城运输与供水生命线的大运河已无需绕道洛阳。如何裁弯取直，让运河从富庶的江南直达北京，成为横亘在新都城前面的新难题。

At this time, the Grand Canal, which was designed as the lifeline of transportation and water supply for capital, no longer needed to bypass the old capital Luoyang. How to cut the bend and straighten it so that the canal can reach Beijing directly from the prosperous places south of the Yangtze River became a priority for the rulers.

　　最终，河北邢台的科学家郭守敬拿出了破解之道。"上知天文，下晓地理"是郭守敬的真实写照。历时数载，勘察地形、寻找水源、计算落差，郭守敬绘出了大运河裁弯取直的线路图，提出了大运河"弃弓走弦"的整体构想，在山东修建运河，连通河北、江苏，实现京、杭直航。

　　In the end, Guo Shoujing a scientist from Xingtai of Hebei Province came up with a solution. "The all-knowing and all-seeing" was almost not an exaggerating compliment for Guo Shoujing on his scientific knowledge. After several years of prospecting of water beneath the terrain and calculating the geographic data, Guo Shoujing came up with the perfect route for the Grand Canal to straighten up. The idea was to build a canal in Shandong to connect Hebei and Jiangsu, making a direct water system between Beijing and Hangzhou.

　　这份设想里也倾注着另一位河北人的心血。沧州水利学家马之贞陪同郭守敬勘查河道，共同破题。在马之贞的主持修建下，1289年，京杭大运河地形高差最大的一段河道——会通河贯通。四年之后，郭守敬主持开凿的北京到通州河段也顺利开通，彻底打通了大运河与都城之间最后的距离，忽必烈震惊于这段河道终点积水潭舳舻蔽水的空前盛况，欣然赐名通惠河。

　　This idea also included efforts made by another native of Hebei. Ma Zhizhen a water conservancy scientist from Cangzhou accompanied Guo Shoujing to investigate the river channel and solved the problem together. Under Ma Zhizhen's supervision, in 1289, Huitong River—the largest construction section of the Beijing-Hangzhou Grand Canal with the largest elevation drop—was completed. Four years later, under Guo Shoujing's supervision, the construction of Beijing-Tongzhou river section was also successfully completed, which removed the final barrier between the Grand Canal and the capital. Kublai Khan was amazed by the unprecedented grand view of the numerous ships on the river near Jishuitan, therefore he named the ending section of the canal Tonghui River.

　　自此，裁弯取直后的京杭大运河全线通航，运河的涟漪，汇聚起了更为广阔的水系。与隋唐大运河相比，航道缩短约900千米。从此，南方的粮食、物资和大量人才都经过这条水路，源源不断地汇聚到北京。

　　Since then, the Beijing-Hangzhou Grand Canal had been opened to navigation. The ripples of the canal had accelerated civilization. Compared with the original Suitang Canal, the river course of this canal was shortened by about 900 kilometers. Since then, food, materials and a large number of talents from the south had traveled through this canal and continuously gathered in Beijing.

有人说，正是因为郭守敬大都治水的成功，奠定这座古城供水与漕运的基础，这座古城的规模才能越来越大。

Some people say that it is because of Guo Shoujing's achievements in regulating the course of the canal in Dadu that laid the foundation of water supply and transportation, providing this ancient city with the opportunity to thrive and grow.

大运河行经八个省市，沿途地貌多样，地势复杂，水向多变。为实现人工工程与天然水道的一体化交通，地形高差、水源控制、水深控制、防洪减灾，每一里河道都写着亟待解决的问题。于是，无数人如同郭守敬一般，殚精竭虑，义无反顾，将毕生所学倾囊而出。他们的光荣，不在史册中的波流水淌，而在河道边的岁月不居。

The Grand Canal passes through eight provinces, encountering various land forms and complex terrains. In order to guarantee a reliable integrated transportation between artificial rivers and natural rivers, engineers had to consider potential problems brought by elevation drops, complex water source, unknown water depth, flood and disaster risks. Every mile of the river needed to be carefully analyzed. As a result, countless people put lifetime efforts into it, just as Guo Shoujing did. Their sacrifice and glory might not have been written in history book, but definitely live along the flowing rivers forever.

世界文化遗产

　　"长河日暮乱烟浮，红叶萧萧两岸秋。夜半不知行近远，一船明月过沧州。"这是清代人孙谔的疑惑。在运河上行船，走了多半夜都没能走出沧州。这不是艺术夸张，很可能是事实。

　　"The long river stretches along the sunset, accompanied by red leaves dwindling on both shores. Under the night sky you know not how far you have traveled, until the moonlight shines at Cangzhou." This is a description by Sun E a poet in the Qing Dynasty, saying that even after spending almost a whole night traveling by water, the boat still has not gone out of Cangzhou. This is not an artistic exaggeration, but most likely a fact.

　　南运河多弯道，仅沧州市全域内就有230多个大弯，最著名的是沧州市区的"Ω"弯。粗略估计，这个弯道比直道多出至少40分钟的航行时间。

　　The South Canal has many turns. In Cangzhou City alone, there are more than 230 major turns. The most famous one is the "Ω" turn in Cangzhou City. A rough estimate suggests that sailing along this turn cost 40 minutes more than sailing on a straight line.

　　修建费力，航行费时，古人这么做是为了解决地势落差。从山东德州四女寺水利枢纽到河北沧州东光县连镇的谢家坝，直线距离仅有52千米，却有着4米的落差。增加弯道，延长河道，从而缓解水势对堤坝的冲击力，这就是俗话说的"三弯抵一闸"。

It was laborious to build and time-consuming to navigate along these canal turns. However, the ancient people designed the canal in this way to avoid elevation drops. From the Sinv Temple hydro-junction in Dezhou of Shandong to Xiejia Dam in Cangzhou of Hebei, the straight-line distance is only 52 kilometers, but there is an elevation drop of four meters. Therefore, engineers decided to add turns and lengthen the river to alleviate the impact of the water pressure on the dam, which illustrates the saying of "three turns save a dam."

　　于是，从四女寺到谢家坝排布着87个大弯，河道也延长到了95千米。这让大运河看起来柔肠百结，婉转旖旎，科学与美学就这样以和谐统一的面目示人。

As a result, 87 big turns were arranged between Sinv Temple and Xiejia Dam, extending the river channel to 95 kilometers. This makes the Grand Canal look indirect but artistic and extremely beautiful, which is an interesting outcome combining science and aesthetics.

只是如此一来，大运河弯道的顶端，就成了承受水势最多的一段，也就是大运河上的险工。自然，这里也是前人展示智慧与技术的所在。

But only because of the design of turns, the top points of the turns have become the section that bears the biggest water pressure, which make it the hardest part of work during construction. However, this was a so where ancient wisdom and technology were displayed.

谢家坝就是这样一处险工。谢家坝也称糯米坝，这个名称透露出它坚固的秘密。历史上，谢家坝曾多次决口。清末，一位姓谢的乡绅，捐资购入上万斤糯米。将黄土、白灰与糯米浆按一定比例混合，这本是修建城池时填补砖缝所用的糯米砂浆。风干后，强度高、韧性大、防渗性好，可以说是古代的超级混凝土。谢家坝这座长218米、高5米、厚3.6米的防洪大堤，就用这种糯米砂浆逐层夯筑而成。

Xiejia Dam was such a demanding project. Xiejia Dam was also called "glutinous rice dam", which revealed its secret of firmness. In the past, Xiejia Dam had burst many times. At the end of the Qing Dynasty, a squire with a surname Xie donated money to buy tens of thousands of catties of glutinous rice. By mixing the loess, white lime and glutinous rice slurry all together in a certain proportion, people created a glutinous rice mortar, which was usually used for fixing brick cracks during castle wall constructions. After air-drying, it was of high intensity, high hardness and good impermeability. It was the ancient super concrete. The Xiejia Dam, a 218-meter-long, 5-meter-high and 3.6-meter-thick flood control embankment, was built with this glutinous rice mortar layer by layer.

　　经过流水冲刷与岁月洗礼，已经很少有人知道，谢家坝沧桑斑驳的外表下竟然蕴藏着无比坚强的内心。

　　After being washed and baptized by running water for years, Xiejia Dam still maintains a strong heart under its mottled appearance and vicissitudes.

　　挑水坝位于衡水市故城县郑口镇，六座形态各异的堤坝，两两间隔二三十米，当地人有个形象的称呼叫龙尾埽。在这里，凸出的堤坝不再默默承受水势冲击，而是以一种进攻的姿态，迎着水势直面一击，起到很大的消减作用。六这个数目，则是在对抗中达成的平衡，水冲一段堤，加修一座坝，一直修到第六座，才抑息止澜，换得两岸平安。

Tiaoshui Dam is located in Zhengkou Town, Gucheng County of Hengshui City. There are six dams of different shapes, twenty to thirty meters apart in pairs. Local people call them the "dragon swing tails." Here, the protruding dams no longer bear the impact of water silently and passively, but face the attack in an offensive posture, which plays a great role in reducing the water impact pressure on canal courses. The number of six is the balance achieved through confrontation experience. Whenever the water rushed a section of the dike, a dam was then built, until the sixth dam was built did the rush stop.

大运河北 世界文化遗产

这是一艘在沧州东光县发掘出来的北宋时期的沉船，剥去千年的淤积，可以窥见它当日的模样。船舱由多个隔舱组成，被发现时装载着磁州窑烧制的瓷器。这也是大运河上最常见的一种货船。

This is a sunken ship from the Northern Song Dynasty excavated in Dongguang County of Cangzhou City. After stripping off the sediment of thousands of years, one can see what it looked like in the past. The cabin consists of multiple compartments and was found to be loaded with porcelain made in Cizhou. This is also the most common type of cargo ship on the Grand Canal.

据记载，大运河最大可通行100吨级船队。"北运河上，舟行船泊，首尾相连。扬帆竖千樯，绵延几十里。满载粮船，逆流而上。"

According to records, the maximum of ship load allowed on the Grand Canal was 100 tons. "On the North Canal, ships and boats are lined up end-to-end, stretching a line for a dozen of miles. The ships are loaded with grain and traveling upstream."

即使是长江这样的大江大河，也有枯水期的行船限制。大运河能做到漕运四季如常，是因为它掌握了调蓄水量密码——闸和减河。

Even a mighty river like the Yangtze River has strict restrictions on ship load during dry seasons. The Grand Canal can transport as usual in all seasons because it has mastered the secret of regulating and storing water—sluice and river reduction.

以前，河北段运河的水源，主要来自燕山与太行山所孕育的河流。漳河、卫河、汶水、泗水以及黄河补充南运河，而北运河离不开永定河和通惠河，通惠河则依靠白浮泉等泉水支持。

In the past, the water source of the Canal in the Hebei section mainly came from the rivers nurtured by Yanshan Mountains and Taihang Mountains. The Zhanghe River, Weihe River, Wenshui River, Sishui River and the Yellow River complement the South Canal, while the North Canal is inseparable from the Yongding River and the Tonghui River, and the Tonghui River is supported by springs such as Baifu Spring.

运河沿线各地地势高低不同，"水往低处流"，运河需要闸来调节流量和方向。通州海拔低于大都近20米，沿着通惠河设有24座船闸，每10里一处，每处建有上下闸门2座，闸门相距1里，调节各段的水量，以使船只能够逆流而上。

The terrain along the Canal is different. "Water flows downwards." The canal needs floodgates to adjust its flow and direction. Tongzhou is nearly 20 meters lower than Dadu. There are 24 ship locks along the Tonghui River, one in every 5 kilometers. One upper and one lower lock gates are built in each place, 500 meters apart, to adjust the water flow so that the ships can travel upstream.

减河，即分流的河道。沧州市区的南边，建有南运河的捷地分洪闸和捷地减河。

River reduction is to create distributaries of the river to divide the current. On the south of Cangzhou City, there are the Jiedi floodgate and Jiedi Distributary of the South Canal.

明弘治三年，这里开挖减河，建桥设闸。此后也多有修缮。据说，清代乾隆帝曾三次亲临现场视察捷地减河分水工事，并为大运河题字立碑。这里的乾隆御碑是中国运河史上的唯一。

In the third year of Hongzhi in the Ming Dynasty, distributaries were excavated here. Bridges and gates were built. There have been many innovations since then. It is said that Emperor Qianlong of the Qing Dynasty visited the site three times to inspect the distributary fortifications of the Jiedi River, where he inscribed for the project and set up a monument for the Grand Canal. The Qianlong Imperial Stele here is the only stele in the history of Chinese canals.

捷地的分洪闸与减河配合使用，枯水期闭闸存蓄河水，保证通航需要。汛期可开闸放水，分洪入减河，保证行船安全。

The floodgates in Jiedi were used in conjunction with distributaries. Gates were closed during the dry season to store the river water to ensure the navigation needs. During the flood season, gates were opened to release water, and the flood could be diverted into distributaries to ensure the safety of boats.

这段几近失传的声音，是华北运河上古老的船工号子，它曾经响彻帆樯如林的运河两岸。如今，这些老人重新演绎的船工号子，让人们重拾关于运河繁忙的记忆。

This almost-lost voice is a boatmen work song on the North China Canal in ancient times, which once resounded along the banks of the Canal. Today, the boatmen work song reinterpreted by these old people has brought back memories of the busy days on the Canal.

当年，伴随着船工号子，大运河成为整个国家不可或缺的经济命脉。明、清两代每年都有大约400万石漕粮经大运河运到北京。

At that time, along with the boatmen work song, the Grand Canal became an indispensable economic lifeline for the entire country. In the Ming and the Qing Dynasties, about 400 million kilograms of tribute grains were transported to Beijing through the Grand Canal every year.

　　邢台市清河县油坊码头，曾经舟来船往，商贾云集，是河北清河、威县、南宫、故城以及山东高唐、夏津等地的商品集散地。今天，油坊古镇不到1000米的河道内，粮食码头、运盐码头等六座码头的遗址仍在，共同诉说着当年商贸往来的繁华。

The Youfang Pier in Qinghe County of Xingtai City used to be a busy hub where ships and merchants gathered to trade. It was a commodity distribution center for places such as Qinghe, Weixian, Nangong and Gucheng in Hebei; Gaotang and Xiajin in Shandong. Today, the ruins of six piers including grain pier and salt transportation pier are still next to the river less than 1,000 meters away from the ancient town of Youfang, telling stories of a bustling past.

　　明清时期，海盐的生产力大大提高，水运成为重要途径。油坊码头的河岸之上，建于道光年间的益庆和盐店是当年的存盐货场，在这里可以一探大运河盐运的过往。

During the Ming and the Qing Dynasties, the production of sea salt was greatly improved. Rivers and ships became an important transportation tool. On the river bank of the Youfang Pier, one can visit the salt storage yard of Yiqinghe Salt House built in the Daoguang period, which could prove the glorious history of salt transportation.

　　盐商是世袭的特权，每次交易需向官方缴税，领取凭证后再到指定盐场买盐，最后运到特定地区销售。益庆和盐店的货品来自渤海之滨的长芦盐场，进出货皆是通过运河。不同于其他码头，油坊的盐运码头在堤坝之上多开了一个涵洞。盐船到达之后，挑夫可以穿过涵洞，直接将盐运到盐店，不再上下河堤，这是人们在劳动中打磨出的与运河相处的智慧。

Salt merchants were hereditary privileges. Each transaction was required to pay taxes to the ruling government. After receiving the tax certificate from the government, they brought it to the designated salt farm to buy salt, and finally shipped it to a designated area for sale. The salts of Yiqinghe Salt House came from the Changlu Salt Field on the coast of the Bohai Sea, and all salts were shipped through the Canal. Different from other piers, Youfang Pier had a culvert exit above the dam. After the salt boats arrived, porters could go through the culvert and transport the salt directly to the salt shops, without going up and down through the river bank. This is wisdom created by people getting along with the Canal.

沿清河县油坊镇南下30千米，是邢台市临西县，这片沃土同样贯穿着来自大运河的千年记忆。临西运河边有一座历经岁月剥蚀的砖窑遗址，考古工作者在这里发掘出大量刻有"嘉靖年间"字样的贡砖，这仅仅是明代临西县八百亩紫禁城贡砖烧制基地的冰山一角。

Thirty kilometers south of Youfang Town in Qinghe County is Linxi County of Xingtai City. This fertile soil also carried a thousand-year memory from the Grand Canal. There was a brick kiln site next to the Linxi Canal. It has been eroded over the years. Archaeologists have found large numbers of tribute bricks engraved with the words "Jiajing Year" here. This is only a tip of the iceberg among the 130-acre brick kiln firing base of the Forbidden City in Linxi County in the Ming Dynasty.

今天，在临西县陈窑村，我们仍能寻觅到这项传承至今的古法技艺。临西贡砖的原料是当地特有的"莲花土"，红、白、黄相间，细腻无杂质。经过碎土、澄泥、制坯等工序，黏土化为砖坯，开始有了金属质感。七天炉火的淬炼，两个月的光阴催化，砖块成了艺术品，每一块的侧边之上还会刻下独有的烙印。沿着大运河，贡砖来到尽头，在当时这个国家最核心的地方构建起另一处传奇。

Today, in Chenyao Village of Linxi County, one can still find this ancient technique that has been passed down to this day. The raw material of Linxi tribute bricks was the unique local "lotus soil". It was delicate and free of impurities with mixing colors of red, white and yellow. After the process of crushing soil, clearing mud, and making blanks, the clay was turned into bricks, and started to have a metallic texture. Seven days of hardening in the furnace, two months of natural catalyzing, the bricks became works of art, and each piece would be engraved with a unique brand on the side. Along the Grand Canal, these tribute bricks traveled to their final destination in the capital, where they continued their legendary story at the core of the nation at that time.

　　"城中烟火千家集，江上帆樯万斛来。"鼎盛时期，卫运河两岸炉窑有数百座。一块小小的砖，一条流经的河，浸润着临西的过去与未来。

　　"Along with the shines of countless fire furnaces in the town, thousands of ships travel across the river." During its heyday, there were hundreds of furnaces and kilns on both banks of the Wei Canal. These small bricks and the river carrying them tell the past and future of Linxi.

　　运河的波光涌动中，船桨摇曳出南来北往的盛世繁华，水流应和着城市街巷的人声熙攘。迎来送往中，繁忙的码头渐渐成了繁华的城市。

Along the waves of the Canal, ships and paddles swayed out of the image of prosperity connecting the south and north. And the river sound sings in harmony with the bustling voices of city streets. Time goes by, the busy pier has gradually become a busy city.

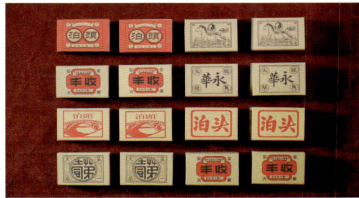

泊头，本是一个码头。20世纪，它被人熟知却是因为火花。火花就是火柴盒的贴画，方寸之间，变幻出一个琳琅满目的世界。紧靠运河，东西又有官道通过，处在水陆十字交叉地带的泊头，在明清时期就是商贸集镇。1911年，泊镇站随津浦铁路通车而设立，泊头的火柴、冶炼铸造、雕版印刷等工业品沿着铁路走向全国。

"Botou" was originally a name of a pier. In the last century, it was well known for the flash of light. The sticker of the matchbox was the image of spark. Historic stories have been packed into these square-inch matchboxes. Botou was close to the Canal, and there were official roads passing through it from east to west. Since it was located in the intersection of river and land, Botou was a trade market town in the Ming and the Qing Dynasties. In 1911, Bozhen Station was established along with the opening of the Tianjin-Shanghai Railway. Industrial products such as matches, smelting and casting, engraving and printing in Botou were brought to the whole country along the railway.

大名古城，是一座因运河而兴盛、因运河改道而黯淡的古城。地处隋唐大运河的重要节点，交通十分便利。五代时，大名古城不仅是黄河以北的经济中心，也是整个华北地区的工商都会。元代大运河裁弯取直，不再经过大名。失去了水运优势，这座古城的地位远不如以前。

The ancient town of Daming was prosperous because of the Canal and it became dimmed because of the diversion of the Canal. It was located at an important node of the Suitang Canal, which provided convenient transportation. During the Five Dynasties, the ancient town of Daming was not only the economic center north of the Yellow River, but also the industrial and commercial center of the entire North China. In the Yuan Dynasty, the Grand Canal changed its course and no longer passed through Daming. Losing the advantage of water transportation, the fame of this ancient town was far outshone than before.

　　大运河沟通的不只是国内的漕运，更是联结世界的活水，它是古代丝绸之路的重要一环。马克思的著作中曾经提到，在中国，江南的茶叶走海路到天津，再走河运到通州，接着走陆路到张家口，远销俄罗斯。

The Grand Canal not only connected domestic water transportation, but also connected the world, as it was an important part of the ancient Silk Road. In Marx's writings, it was mentioned that in China, tea from regions south of the Yangtze River traveled to Tianjin by sea, then to Tongzhou by river, and then to Zhangjiakou by land, where it was exported to Russia.

大运河
世界文化遗产

馆陶，以陶为名，源自这里盛产的一种黑陶。陶器是人类最早利用化学变化改变一种物质天然性质的开端。馆陶黑陶历史悠久，以当地优质黏土为主，借助独特的工艺，让弥漫在窑里的浓烟将碳粒渗入坯体而呈黑色，质地细腻，形体素雅。这种黑陶，连同太行山东麓定窑、井陉窑、邢窑、磁州窑出产的瓷器，还有河北平原出产的丝绸，经大运河，从黄骅海丰镇的古代海港走向世界，传播着中国之美。

Guantao was well known for its pottery, a kind of black pottery that originated here. Pottery was the first product made by human beings to use chemical reactions to alter the natural properties of a substance. Guantao black pottery has a long history and is mainly made of local high-quality clay. The unique craftsmanship allows the dense smoke in the kiln penetrates the green body with carbon particles to turn it black, with fine texture and elegant shape. This black pottery, together with the porcelain produced in Ding kiln, Jingxing kiln, Xing kiln and Cizhou kiln at the eastern foot of Taihang Mountains, and the silk produced in Hebei Plain, traveled from the ancient seaport in Haifeng Town of Huanghua to the world via the Grand Canal, advertising the beauty of China.

大运河日夜不息，两岸文化奔涌向前。一河碧水里，劳动人民的勇气与智慧演变成技艺与艺术。它们沿河而行，汇聚、交融，迸发出了更炫目的光彩，成为经久不衰的文化符号。

The Grand Canal never stopped to rest, pushing cultures on shores to thrive. With the help of beautiful river, the courage and wisdom of the working people evolved into skills and art. They traveled along the river, gathered and exchanged, yielding more splendor and becoming an enduring cultural symbol.

沧州吴桥县宋家院村，大运河的转弯，让河滩有了状如耳朵的轮廓，这是吴桥倾听世界的样子。

In Songjiayuan Village in Wuqiao County of Cangzhou, the huge turn of the Grand Canal gives the shoreline an ear-like shape, as if that is how Wuqiao listens to the voice of the world.

　　吴桥是闻名世界的杂技之乡，据说从汉代开始就演练杂技。隋唐以来，沿着大运河这条黄金水道，吴桥杂技艺人北上南下，远涉重洋。明末清初时，吴桥杂技艺人遍布50多个国家，以绝活儿征服世界，他们的名头与运河的波光交相辉映，成为蜚声中外的杂技军团。

Wuqiao is a world-famous hometown of acrobatics. It is said that acrobatics have been practiced since the Han Dynasty. Since the Sui and the Tang Dynasties, along the golden waterway of the Grand Canal, Wuqiao acrobats traveled north and south, and across the ocean. In the late Ming and early Qing Dynasties, Wuqiao acrobats spread over more than 50 countries and amazed the world with their unique skills. Their fame and the waves of the Canal add radiance to each other, and thus they became the legion of acrobatics well known at home and abroad.

大运河滋养了吴桥，杂技打开了吴桥与世界往来的大门。如今，两年一届的中国吴桥国际杂技艺术节汇聚起全世界的杂技爱好者，曾经沿着运河走向世界的吴桥杂技，与世界一起构建一个文化交流、美美与共的艺术殿堂。

The Grand Canal has nourished Wuqiao, and acrobatics have opened the door for Wuqiao to communicate with the world. Today, the biennial China Wuqiao International Acrobatic Art Festival brings together acrobatics lovers from all over the world. Wuqiao acrobatics, which once went to the world along the canal, has built an art palace of cultural exchange and shared beautiful world.

岸边的喧闹并未分散大运河的注意力，运送着南来北往的船只，一如千年来的日常。只是，在更广阔的时空里，变革的浪潮开始涌动，运河的命运也随之变化。

The bustles on the shore did not distract the Grand Canal from transporting ships to their destinations for a thousand years. However, on a wider scale of history, the tides of reform begin to appear and the fate of the canal also changes with it.

　　1901年，漕运废止，大运河南北断流。不久铁路兴起，机车更迭，陆运开始繁忙。曾经南船北马的大运河逐渐被遗忘在了岁月里。到20世纪70年代，河北境内的大运河不再具备通航能力。失去了河水的大运河，空旷、寂寥，如同一段被遗失的记忆。

　　In 1901, water transportation was abolished, and the Grand Canal was cut off between the North and South. Soon after the rise of railways, land transportation became busy. The once busy Grand Canal was gradually forgotten. By the 1970s, the Hebei section of the Grand Canal was no longer navigable. The Grand Canal which had lost its water was empty and alone, like a lost memory.

　　岁月流转，历史终将掀开新的一页。2008年，南运河开始了它的新使命，用它的河道为南水北调东线输水。输水，就此成为南运河今后的重要功能。曾经的黄金水道，在新时代又开始了新的作为。

　　As time goes by, history would eventually turn to a new page. In 2008, the South Canal started its new mission, using its channel to transport water resources to the eastern route of the South-to-North Water Diversion Project. Water resource diversion has thus become an important function of the South Canal. The once golden waterway has been assigned a new mission in the new era.

　　浸润在这方水土的血脉中，对于运河人来说，这条运河是奔腾在心灵河床上的精神源头，更是他们生活与梦想的一部分。

For people who have lived by the Grand Canal, the canal is the spiritual source that resonates with their soul. What's more, it is a part of their life and dream.

　　调水、治水、整修河道，如今，大运河北京段40千米、河北段20千米皆已通航，不久的将来，河北人坐着游船入北京，重现大运河兴盛的情形。

　　Water transfer, water control and river repairs have been carried out. Today, the 40-kilometer Beijing section of the Grand Canal and the 20-kilometer Hebei section are open to navigation again. In the near fu ure, people of Hebei will be able to go to Beijing on cruise ships and the prosperity of the Grand Canal will be re-shown.

　　奔涌的河水沿着北运河一路南下，在静静流淌中守护着美丽的家园。历史更迭向前，跳动的涟漪唤醒了运河两岸的无限魅力。

　　The surging river flows south all the way along the North Canal, guarding the beautiful homeland. As time goes by, the beating ripples awaken the infinite charm of both banks along the canal.

河为线，城为珠，2017年，大运河国家文化公园建设拉开帷幕。河水似乎从来没有这么欢快过。

The canal is a line and cities are pearls. In 2017, the construction of the Grand Canal National Cultural Park was begun. The river never seemed to have been so cheerful.

香河运河文化公园、沧州大运河绿色长廊、故城运河风情公园、东光县氧生园运动休闲森林公园，每一米河段打造着自己的专属风情；每一个古镇都在寻找曾经独有的特色。曾经与河相宜的人居环境，独特的建筑风格，精湛的手工技艺都在这里一一被唤醒、重生。

Xianghe Canal Cultural Park, Cangzhou Grand Canal Green Corridor, Gucheng Canal Park, Dongguang County Oxygen Park Sports and Leisure Forest Park—each meter of the river is creating its own unique charm; every ancient town is looking for a unique style to commemorate the past. The amazing living environment, the unique architectural style and the exquisite craftsmanship are all awakened and reborn here one after another.

曾经遇水而兴的水利文化、漕运文化、船舶文化、商事文化、饮食文化在河畔有了依托，随水流传的民间艺术与民俗也有迹可循。失而复得的美好，重现水的魅力，重塑两岸风貌，大运河也在重写人与河的关系。

The water conservancy culture, canal transportation culture, ship culture, commercial culture and food culture that once flourished on account of being by the water find their home on the river banks to rely on. And there are also traces of folk art and folk customs that passed along the water. The recovered glory is presenting the charm of water and the scenery on both banks. The Grand Canal is also rewriting the relationship between man and river.

见证过中国悠久的历史文明，展览着中国古代科技与文化的灿烂，流淌着民族的记忆与精神的基因，大运河这首由无数中国人接续奋斗，在两千年岁月里写就的史诗，永远是人类历史上的伟大奇迹。

The canal has witnessed China's long history and civilization, exhibited the splendor of ancient Chinese science and culture, and flowed with the memory and spiritual genes of the nation. The Grand Canal, an epic written by countless Chinese people who have been striving for two thousand years, will always be a great miracle in human history.

这些陈列在大地上，永不褪色的世界文化遗产，承载着灿烂文明，传承着历史文化，维系着民族精神，今天，它们在创造性转化和创新性发展中愈发地生动、鲜活。文物在说话，历史在说话，文化在说话，它们正在为实现中华民族伟大复兴的中国梦凝聚起磅礴力量！

These unfading world cultural heritages displayed on the earth carry splendid civilization, inherit history and culture, and maintain the national spirit. Today, they shine again in creative transformation and innovative development. Cultural relics are speaking; history is speaking; culture is speaking. They are gathering great majestic power to bring about the great rejuvenation of the Chinese nation and realize the Chinese dream!